RELEASING THE POWER WITHIN THROUGH Spiritual Dynamics

The Genius of Jesus REVEALED

ISBN - 0-9678132-0-4

Contents

Acknowledgments

This book is the result of the faith, prayers and hard work of many individuals!

I am forever grateful to my father, the late Deacon Samuel Wilson, and my mother, Lovey Wilson, who both through their fearless pursuit of truth, justice and righteousness, bequeathed a legacy to me to inspire and motivate my generation.

I am also grateful to the members and supporters of the Union Temple Baptist Church, whose constant prayers and loyalty provide me with much strength.

For the development and production of this book, I feel a deep sense of gratitude to:

> My wife, Rev. Mary L. Wilson, and my family who time and again anxiously inquired about the progress of this work and were always there to encourage me.
>
> My administrative secretary, Norma Roy-Hooks who typed the original manuscript.
>
> My executive administrative assistant, Michele Roberts, who handled all of my special correspondence requests and inquiries.
>
> Adama Melitte, chief editor of this work, who did a yeoman's effort in identifying and correcting errors of every divers and sundry sort.
>
> Dr. Gene Rice, Dr. Evans Crawford, and Dr. Cain Hope Felder, all professors at Howard University School of Divinity who critiqued this work and offered invaluable comments and suggestions.
>
> Protean Gibril, my gifted advisor and co-publisher, who helped me to get this work out in a timely fashion.
>
> Minister Eric Kareem, Dick Gregory, and Tony Bowder, all of whom assisted me in my research.
>
> And finally to Almighty God - the giver of every good and perfect gift!

Thank You! Thank You! Thank You!

About the Author

Reverend Willie F. Wilson

Chief Nana Kwadwo Boafo I

Born in Newport News, Virginia, He received his bachelor's degree in Journalism from Ohio University. Reverend Wilson also attended Howard University School of Divinity where he received a master's degree and did his doctoral studies. He was the recipient of several awards including the Rockefeller Protestant Fellowship Award for academic achievement and the Vernon Johns Preaching Award for the most "Outstanding Orator and Preacher" of his graduating class. His repertoire includes training in self-evaluation techniques and psychiatric counseling under the esteemed instruction of Dr. B. Haldane and Dr. Ernest Bruder.

In 1980 Reverend Wilson was ordained a Wolof priest in the Gambia, West Africa and with this honor he has the uttermost credence and positive authority to perform any and all ceremonies relating to African people at home and abroad. He was inducted in this high ceremony as Nana Kwadwo BOAFO I. Chief Nana Kwadwo Boafo I has performed scores of African-American weddings and was referenced in the book *Jumping the Broom.* In 1994, Rev Wilson published his first book, *The African-American Wedding Manual.* In October 1993 in a ceremony at Asankrangwa, Western Ghana, a stool was created by the Asankare-Bretuo clan to be occupied by Willie F. Wilson, the new subchief. Union Temple Baptist Church has erected a home in Ghana, West Africa for its rites of passage programs. The church has donated over one million dollars in medical supplies to the hospital in Asankrangwa, sponsors an adopt-a-child educational program and is engaged in several business enterprises in Africa including gold mining and brick manufacturing.

Pastor Wilson was recognized by USA Newspaper as one of the ten most valuable people in America in 1986.

Drawing upon his African heritage and contemporary economics, Reverend Wilson has pastored Union Temple Baptist Church for more than 25 years. With more than 6,500 members the church has distinguished itself with an elaborate investment program that has funneled more than $10,000,000 into housing, education and health services. The church operates a home for teenagers, a rehabilitation program for substance abusers, a feeding program for the hungry and a pioneer rites of passage program for youth and adults. A new independent recording label called *UT Records* was recently initiated. Union Temple Baptist Church was nominated by the National Conference of Black Churchmen, an organization of over 68,000 churches, as one of the 100 Model Black Churches in America. In 1997 Pastor Wilson and Union Temple Baptist Church were awarded the President's Service Award by President Bill Clinton. This is the most prestigious presidential recognition given for community service. Of the 3,500 nominations and 41 finalists the church was one of only 16 national organizations to receive plaques and sterling silver White House medallions. The church has received world acclaim for its 30 x 19 foot mural depicting *The Last Supper*. This mural is believed to be the first of its kind. It depicts not only the Black Christ but the twelve disciples as twelve significant Africans and African-Americans; among them Martin Luther King, Jr., Rosa Parks, Nelson Mandela, and Malcolm X.

Rev. Wilson led former Mayor Marion Barry in the most spirited political resurrection in the history of American politics with an unthinkable reelection to the Office of Mayor of Washington, DC in 1995.

He also has led his church for the last 17 years in the organization of Unifest, one of the largest cultural arts festivals on the east coast, which annually attracts over 250,000 people over a two day span.

This distinguished pastor, orator, lecturer and teacher is listed among Who's Who in African American Leadership. He is a noted scholar and recognized authority on Africentric theology.

Rev. Wilson has recently been elected to the Board of Trustees of the University of the District of Columbia.

Reverend Wilson has been featured in many top publications and has appeared on numerous television shows. He has spoken at universities throughout the nation and has traveled extensively as a spiritual advisor to persons such as the former South African President Nelson Mandela, former DC Mayor Marion Barry, and World Heavyweight Champion Riddick Bowe.

As a national committee member and executive producer of the

Million-Man March, Pastor Wilson orchestrated the successful assembly of over 100,000 men from the Washington, DC area. He is the owner of the historic Pyramid Bookstore building, located near Howard University where a 13x5 foot sculpture of an ancient Egyptian is on the facade as created by world renown Ethiopian sculptor Falaka Yima.

Reverend Wilson is married to Rev. Mary Lewis Wilson of Buffalo, New York and is the proud father of two sons and two daughters.

Foreword

"Who is worthy to break the seals and open the scroll?" But no one in heaven or on earth or under the earth could open the scroll or even look inside it. I wept and wept because no one was found who was worthy to open the scroll or look inside. Then one of the elders said to me, "Do not weep! See, the Lion of the tribe of Judah, the Root of David, has triumphed. He is able to open the scroll and its seven seals."

(Rev.5:2-5)

The challenge that has persistently faced African-Americans over the last 400 years is the question of how do we regain true freedom. The question has been raised consistently by politicians, activists, scholars, religious leaders warriors and at some level by every African-American person who has attained the age of discernment since our kidnapping and enslavement in America. The early rebels such as Harriet Tubman believed that freedom was a physical journey to an area where physical captivity was not enforced by law. Warriors like Nat Turner believed that revolt against the captor would release the captives. Later, abolitionists like Fredrick Douglas devoted their lives to changing the laws that prohibited the freedom of African people. Throughout most of the 20th century, the effort was made to seek freedom by challenging the American laws and traditions that maintained inequality and kept freedom out of our reach. Through all of these phases, there has been the predominant belief that prayer, faith and patience would eventually send a Divine Savior who would restore freedom to the captive African people in America.

As the end of the 20th century approached, increasingly there was a growing recognition that these strides toward freedom were stages but real freedom must be achieved by inner attainment and not as an external achievement. Freedom can only be restored when people are able to free their minds. With this realization, preachers, scholars, politicians, educators and others began to focus their attention on the issue of how should the captives free their minds. The answer to this question has remained elusive, as has the proverbial search for freedom, because the tools for freeing our minds have remained the tools given to us by our captors. Many of those tools have been intellectual ones heralded by multitudes of educators that "education is the key to freedom." The insights of scholars such as Dr. Carter G. Woodson have revealed the irony that often the most educated have been the least effective in furthering the cause of freedom. The intellectual tools that they have acquired have often served to "miseducate" them and render then impotent in pursuit of their own freedom. Education has changed the surface appearance of our captivity but structurally the goal of freedom has remained elusive.

In recent years, an increasing number of scholars have begun to challenge the nature of the educational tools that we have been working with and have argued the need for tools that "center" us in our reality as the subject matter of our educational objectives. This effort has led to the development of Africentric scholarship as the paradigm of choice if education is to help us to free our minds. There remains an absence of consensus as to what "Africentricity" really is, but the concept represents an attempt to shift a paradigm of learning that only equips us to perpetuate our own captivity.

In addition to education, the other major tool that has been used to restore freedom is religion. Certainly, more African-Americans have attempted to use these tools (particularly of the Christian faith) more than those who have tried to use the educational "keys" to freedom. Unfortunately, millions of devout Christians have remained just as powerless and subjugated as were their great grandparents on America's plantations because of the limitations in the religious tools. It seemed the "scroll" containing the formula for freedom was sealed as firmly as was the scroll described in the book of Revelations that is quoted above. This important volume, *Releasing the Power Within through Spiritual Dynamics* by Rev. Willie Wilson, represents a valuable set of keys to open the sealed scroll to our mental and spiritual freedom. Rev. Wilson presents to us an analysis of why the tool of religion, as we have understood it, has not worked to bring us freedom and then carefully delineates how the key must be used in order to open the seals on the scrolls. The ideas that are revealed in this masterpiece are precision instruments but they must be exchanged for the inadequate tools that we have been using. Of course, to challenge those archaic and useless tools brings the Message bearer into conflict with protectors of the established but useless tools.

The power that is released through the spiritual dynamics described by Rev. Wilson opens several important seals on the concealed scrolls that we have been using. The first important key that he presents is our definition of who we are. In his clear and penetrating description of our true human identity as spiritual entities who are carriers of the mark of God, he challenges conventional religious and psychological understanding of who we are. His discussion is compelling, well-documented and immediately liberates us from the limiting notions that we have of ourselves as material creatures or lost souls who must find an external God to save us. Rev. Wilson immediately empowers us through his analysis and scriptural support that shows that mental and spiritual freedom is our very nature and neither requires messianic intervention nor the benevolence of those who captured our bodies. We have found "freedom land" as soon as we realize who and what we are.

Another seal that is broken by Rev. Wilson's penetrating discussion is the power of religion as revealed through scripture. Rev. Wilson boldly challenges the established church's reliance on dead-letter (useless words without meaning) scripture. His examples show how the concrete interpretation and mistranslation of scriptural insights have made the scriptures of revealed religion to be tools that have sealed our captivity rather than a vehicle of our liberation. Through his "spiritual dynamics " he unleashes the power of scripture that can only come through clear understanding, relevant application and clear guidance for human action. He shatters the ark of dogmatic misunderstanding whereby people hold onto "the word" without any understanding of what "the word" means. He challenges those who defend the misunderstood word to present the human documentation of peace, healing and ultimately freedom if their "spiritual stagnation" accomplishes what this dynamic spiritual word is able to achieve for the advancement of human life. Rev. Wilson boldly proclaims that scripture should be the interior ornaments that create God consciousness. The awareness that God dwells within us should be the ultimate objective of religion

Certainly, the critical seal that Rev. Wilson breaks on the scroll of human freedom is his successful liberation of the "African Jesus the Christ." The power of spiritual dynamics to free the human mind and spirit is reflected in the successful freeing of Jesus in this powerful and revealing book. In some of the most penetrating illustrations and analyses that have come to us in the course of our captivity, Rev. Wilson releases the "Son of God." He shows how God's son has been incarcerated in mystical, esoteric [symbolic imagery] and hidden on remote islands of human incapability. Jesus as a human being, who found the God that he was created to be and his role as a model to teach all human beings the attainability of the God within themselves, is given back to us. Rev. Wilson resurrects the real Savior in restoring Jesus who is to be emulated as a guide rather than worshipped as an idol. Jesus is made *dynamic* again and in doing so, he is resurrected once again as an example of what human beings can and must do. Though the example used in this volume is the release of the genius of Jesus, Rev. Wilson helps us to release all of the sterling God conscious human examples that have been shrouded by religious idolatry and dogma. As Jesus is freed, so are all of the messengers and examples of human potential freed from their stagnation that comes from their isolation from the human experience. Rev. Wilson offers us real freedom potential when he gives Jesus back his human status and makes his example an attainable model for any human being who will follow his example and fulfill their potential to become the "Sons and Daughters of God" that we were created to be. Rev. Wilson boldly tears down the idols that have made "Christ" a surname rather than an attainable consciousness for all human beings. Spiritual dynamics restores the energy of movement and activity to all Christians and other religious people and puts us on the "freedom road."'

The re-Africanization of Christianity is another seal broken. The cultural alienation of religion that has given African-Americans the aspiration to become other than ourselves in order to achieve the goals of the religion is certainly one of the reasons that despite our multitudinous participation in religion, we have not attained mental nor spiritual freedom. Too many of us have tried to get washed "whiter than snow" as an image of purification, believing that our Blackness disqualified us from perfection. When we discover that religion, scripture, prophethood, miracles, healing and even God is expressed in our own cultural form, then we have access to the empowerment that should come from religion. This is the power that releases us from all limitations and makes us a part of the family of God. We can feel good about who we are and embrace the identity that guides us to become the children of God we were created to be.

Rev. Wilson brings us a wonderful gift. He joins that caravan of freedom fighters who have struggled to help us reclaim our birthright since it was taken away. In a more contemporary context, he is engaged in the purification of religion as the Africentric scholars have been engaged in the purification of education. He is joining the ranks of those remarkable religious thinkers such as Henry McNeil Turner, Howard Thurman, Edward Blyden, Martin Luther King, Jr., Marcus Garvey, Elijah Muhammad and many others who have dared to challenge the status quo and force a paradigm shift. Like these icons of religious thought Rev. Willie Wilson has not only challenged the ideas of the paradigm, but he has challenged the social and political structure of the Old World order. The reason that we must listen to Rev. Wilson's appeals in this volume is because he comes equipped with examples of his highly successful ministry. What he offers in his discussion of "spiritual dynamics" is not a theoretical framework subject to verification, but instead he brings the verification of having reshaped one of the most incorrigible urban communities in America through the application of these ideas. He has reached the hearts and minds of thousands who were held in the bondage of drugs, poverty, political passivity and an array of modern day slave behaviors and has offered them the tools of spiritual dynamics that have freed them from captivity. He has become a formidable political force in the heart of America's national capital because of his practice of what is preached in this book. His personal leadership as the local chair of the Million Man March at the site of its occurrence did much to make this historic event the success that it was. Rev. Wilson has demonstrated the power of spiritual dynamics with the economic, social, psychological and spiritual victories that he has demonstrated in the lives of those who have studied these principles under his inspired leadership. He has achieved international recognition as an agent of change and successful human growth because of his living and teaching these ideas.

So, the proof of what this document offers is not the stagnant promise of a "happy day in the sweet by and by," but he has demonstrated the dynamic success of these principles in changing our world right here and right now. The elusive freedom that we seek as individuals and as a captive community can clearly be attained through the "power within through spiritual dynamics." This book is a timely contribution to our advancement and it should be a required spiritual and mental map to guide us into the next millennium and back to our highest potential as African people, in particular, and as human beings, in general.

Na'im Akbar, Ph.D
Florida State University and
Mind Productions & Associates
Tallahassee, FL.

Theological Review

In this season of change and changing aeons, Willie Wilson, well known for his accomplishments as Pastor, spiritual leader, Africanist, and community activist in the Washington, DC area and around the nation has brought forth a truly seminal book entitled *Releasing the Power Within through Spiritual Dynamics*. This timely major new resource for the Black church inspires, informs, and challenges all of us with the force and combined spirits of Dr. Howard Thurman and Dr. Leon Wright. The book is dedicated to them both, who Wilson acknowledges as most influential in his theological and pastoral formation and his many years of struggle to uplift African American Christians, and others who languish in the margins of society. The imprints of Thurman's *Jesus and the Disinherited* and Wright's *From Cult to Cosmos - Can Jesus Be Saved?* are consistently evident in this book. Both Thurman and Wright were once professors at the Howard University School of Divinity and this book's pages are a fitting tribute to Thurman within the context of the centennial of his birth.

Wilson's *Releasing the Power* is a significant breakthrough in critical, but "user-friendly" Bible, Spirituality and Black Church studies, because in a highly readable, passionate and insightful way, the author celebrates "the genius of Jesus" from the vantage point of Afro-sensitivity and spirituality. In these fast paced, but cogent eight chapters of the book, Brother Wilson offers a new but in another sense very ancient basis of hope for the people of God. No matter what seeks to bedevil us as people of the African diaspora (social-political-economic; whether violence, drugs, oppressive debt, the criminality of the "American justice" system and the like) Wilson reminds us that answers of empowerment can be discerned in the Holy Bible and a wealth of supportive literature. He persuasively commends to us the holistic spirituality of Jesus or, as Professor Wright would say, "The Religion of Jesus rather than the religion about Jesus"! At the same time, he skillfully opens up to the wider Black community many books and other written material which in and of themselves represent a treasure trove for Black Liberation.

I am delighted to endorse this important transforming resource that will assist in shaping an entirely new level of serious discourse at a time when so many Black television evangelists and other mega "praise and worship centers" pay so little attention to the need for new Christian marching orders for a force that can counter both the deceptive materialism and the subtle encroachments upon our people made by empty apologies and the Christian Coalition. This is must reading for Bible Study groups, Pastors and seminarians.

Rev. Cain Hope Felder, Ph.D.
Professor, New Testament Language and Literature
Howard University and Chairman and Director,
The Biblical Institute for Social Change, Inc.

Dedications

This book is dedicated to the many, many students who over the years have taken my class in Spiritual Dynamics.

It is also dedicated posthumously to my mentor, the late Dr. Leon Wright, former professor of New Testament at Howard University School of Divinity. It was he who led me to experience the New Birth of the dynamic indwelling of God.

Lastly, this book is dedicated to Dr. Howard Thurman who opened my eyes to Jesus' "true teachings" to the oppressed.

Preface

In 1949 when Dr. Howard Thurman first published his book, *Jesus and the Disinherited*, he posed the very staving and poignant question about "the significance of the religion of Jesus to people who stand with their backs against the wall [...]."

He went on to state that "it is one emphasis that has been lacking – except where it has been a part of a very unfortunate corruption of the missionary impulse [...]."

Then he raised the question of why Christianity has been so "impotent" in addressing the imbalances and inequities in American society. He further asks whether the impotency is due to the "betrayal of the genius of the religion of Jesus," or is it due to a "basic weakness in the religion itself?"

These questions are just as relevant today, some fifty years later, as they were when Thurman's book was published. I know that some individuals in our disenfranchised community have enjoyed success and prosperity, but the condition of the masses has become increasingly grave in recent years; at the same time there appears to be more churches, more televangelists, more radio broadcasts, and more religious programming and literary exposure than ever before.

And though billions and billions of dollars have been disbursed for social programs through the years, based upon the belief that money would solve the problems, conditions are worse than ever.

If Christ is the answer, then what is the problem? Why, with churches on almost every corner in the African American community extolling the power of God to deliver the masses, are so many people in such bad condition?

Let me first assure those who read this book that there is no intent on my part to undermine the tenuous "racial unity" in America, but something is gravely wrong in this nation that supposedly has as its foundation the Judeo-Christian ethic.

Why are almost 50% of Black males, between the ages of 20-29, either in jail or under some type of law enforcement supervision? Why are there so few men in the home, so that over 65% of African American households are female-headed? Why are 30% of Black male high school graduates and 50% of Black female graduates living below the poverty line defined as a family of four making less than $12,000 a year? Why is it that in most urban areas, where African Americans constitute less than 30% of the population, are they convicted of 60% of the crimes? Why have the masses of African Americans become permanent occupants and residents of the most depressed, devastated real estate in America? Why are African Americans a highly disproportionate number of the homeless? Why do African Americans own less than 1% of the private businesses in America? And the net worth of 40% of African American families is zero or below, why? Why is less than 1% of the stocks and bonds owned by American individuals (not institutions), owned by African Americans?

The larger question to be addressed in this text is the same one raised by Dr. Howard Thurman over 50 years ago. Has Christianity played a role in the ongoing saga of the insidious and all pervasive racism in America? Further, what does the teaching of Jesus offer in the face of such mind-boggling statistics? Is it impotent? Is there hope in Christianity to address the scope and complexity of the problems of oppressed people in America? Has the message and religion of Jesus been properly appropriated, or has there indeed been a betrayal of the genius of Jesus? Is Christianity impotent in the face of these seemingly overwhelming statistics? Is there salvation in Christianity? Not just soul salvation – but is there economic, social, psychological, and spiritual salvation to be found in the religion of Jesus for oppressed people?

I strongly feel that the genius of Jesus has been betrayed and that the genius must be revealed. In this book I pray that you will find the hidden treasure of the Jesus-message which has been effectively obscured and veiled and as Howard Thurman says "muffled" and "distorted" for about the last 1700-1800 years. I do, indeed, strongly feel that I have found an answer that, if discovered by the masses, could turn things around overnight. Some will read this book and find it to be frightening, divisive, controversial, and perhaps even heretical. Some of these angry readers are sincere, even if misguided souls, who fear the kind of serious questioning of the religion about Jesus that we have been "given," which has been falsely labeled as "unadulterated truth" by those who continue to dominate, rule, control, and lord over the masses of oppressed people not only in America, but throughout the world.

I find great solace in the fact that Jesus, Himself, questioned the established religion of His day that He found to be stultifying and stymieing to the masses of oppressed people of His time.

Because I am His follower, He has commissioned me to do no less than He. I must be bold, honest and a witnessing disciple for the welfare of the masses of oppressed people.

What is Spiritual Dynamics

Chapter I

What is Spiritual Dynamics? This book might be aptly called a course in God's school, a school that will prayerfully result in your birth into Godhood, your original true nature. It is a school you graduate *in*, not *from*. This is to say, spiritually, you are always in the process of becoming. There is no defined arrival, no graduation, and no seniority. The dynamics of anything is the way in which it properly functions to manifest its true nature or purpose. Spiritual Dynamics involves the teachings required to achieve perfection, which is the original essence of every human spirit. In the Garden of Eden story (Genesis 2:25) we are told that in the beginning Adam and Eve (Mankind) were "naked... and were not ashamed." This symbolizes the fact that in that perfect, utopian environment, called the Garden of Eden, man in the beginning could stand unembarrassed before the gaze of God. But someway, somehow man lost his connection to God. The dynamics of anything is that "power" ("dunamis" in Greek) that sets something in motion or causes it to function. A good example would be to describe the dynamics of an automobile. The way in which the engine, transmission and other parts of the automobile work together to cause the automobile to move would be the dynamics of the automobile.

At the core of Spiritual Dynamics is a set of observances, teachings, and practices to guide you to achieve a totally successful life through realizing the power of God within you.

The goal in Spiritual Dynamics is to achieve self-knowledge. We must become conscious or aware of our true nature as beings in the image and likeness of God. The goal is to become a Christ, which (literally means an "anointed one") an enlightened being while still alive in the flesh.

Na'im Akbar points out in his book, *The Community of Self,* that:

> The outcomes of self-knowledge are many and affect all aspects of human life. These outcomes can be summarized in three general areas:
>
> (1) Self -acceptance
> (2) Self-help

(3) Self-discovery

> Self-acceptance is the beginning for all positive social activity. Knowing who you are acquaints you with the best of your human potential and leads to a productive acceptance of self.
>
> Self-help [also] has its basis in self-knowledge.... People who know themselves want to fully care for self. Cooperation with others is certainly a part of self-help, but dependency is not.
>
> The final significant outcome of self-knowledge is the drive for self-discovery. "Self-discovery is the fuel for exploration, scholarship and all of the pursuits that guide our actions to ward increasing the store of human information [...]." The boundaries of personal capability are also challenged by this force of self-discovery. The person with limited self-knowledge and consequently a limited drive for self-discovery will be quite complacent. Such a person will accept whatever limited definition he is given about what he can or cannot do.

What do we mean by the word "Spiritual"? The words Spirit and Spiritual in *Webster's 9th Collegiate* edition are derived from the words Spiritus meaning "breath" and Spiritualis 'of breathing of wind' with the preferred definition of Spirit being "the animating or vital principle held to give life to vital organisms."

There is a difference between Spirituality and Religiosity. The term religion comes from the Latin word "Relegéré." The prefix re means to "go back to the original status or position," while legere means "to link, to bind, or to tie to our original source," which is God. Therefore, the essence of religion is that of linking back to our original source, which is God. Psychologists tell us that much of the psychopathology of the human being can be traced to the experience of separateness and the unconscious desire to reconnect with one's mother in the womb. The human remembers the closeness and warmth of the womb and is always trying to re-experience it. Likewise our spirits, having come from God, long to get back to our original status as one with God.

Religion is supposed to be a process of assisting men and women to reconnect with God, our Creator. It is the vehicle, the *means* by which we connect to the source of life. The spirit *is* the source of life.

The Bible in John 4:24 amplifies the fact that worship is foundational to everything else we do in the Christian life. We are told in the story of the Samaritan woman (John 4:23) that God is seeking "true worshippers," and if God is seeking such, then worship must be very valuable. According to Jesus— "An hour is coming, and now is when the true worshippers shall worship the Father in spirit and in truth; for such people the Father seeks to be His worshippers" (John 4:23).

So if worship is so critical – what does it mean to worship God? The word <u>worship</u> in the New Testament in Greek means "to connect." So the verse re-read says, God is a Spirit and those who connect with Him, must do so in spirit and in truth. So God is seeking "true connectors"—people who really, truly understand how to connect with Him. And how do we connect with Him? Jesus the master teacher states that God is Spirit. That means God's essence is not corporeal or physical. God does not have a body. So when we say that God is Spirit, we are saying that He is invisible. So if you are going to worship this invisible God, Jesus says that your worship must arise from within the invisible part of you. You cannot connect (worship) with God with your body alone. Because God is spirit, He operates or deals primarily in the invisible, metaphysical or spiritual realm, not the physical or visible realm. Like begets like. Spirit cannot connect with flesh. Since God is Spirit, man must connect spiritually.

Now to connect with God spiritually these verses further tell us that we must worship (connect) in "spirit" and in "truth". That is to say, to connect with God we must know our true nature as spiritual beings with the temporary loan of a body. Authentic, accurate connecting to God recognizes His spiritual nature and our own spiritual nature. It takes not only the right attitude, but also the right information about our true nature and God's true nature in order to connect (worship) with God. We are spiritual beings on a human journey and not as Stephen Covey states in his book, *The Seven Habits of Highly Effective People*, human beings on a spiritual journey.

A good example of the difference between Spirituality and Religiosity is to describe the function and purpose of a car. A car is a vehicle designed to transport people from one place to another place or destination. A Cadillac is a car, but not the *only* car. A Ford is a car, but only one make or type of car. A Chevrolet is a car, but not the only vehicle that can transport you from one place to your place of destination. The primary function is transportation. It should be noted that the purpose of a vehicle, in the sense of religion, is not to just take you to church. It can be used to run errands, to go shopping, or just to go for a pleasant ride out into the countryside. True practice of religion should guide us in all aspects of our lives. What I am now speaking to is the narrow, provincial view that many of us have which limits religion to only being concerned about our spiritual awareness. Taking this analogy a step further, we should note that cars are not the only mode of transportation. There are buses, airplanes, and trains, all with the ability to transport you from one place to another. Such an understanding of religion prevents one from insisting that only one religion can get us to God.

Based on the performance, a lack of breakdowns and repairs, a particular owner may conclude that his vehicle is the best. That owner is simply trying to describe how wonderfully his vehicle has served in getting him to his destination. So it is with religions. Religions are ways to God, but ours is not the one and only, *exclusive* way. You have often seen an old car with a bumper sticker reading: "I may be slow, but I'm in front of you." The make or model is not important. How old or slow the vehicle is really is of no consequence. All that matters is that it takes you from where you are to your destination. What this means is that the purpose of the vehicle is just to get you to your destination.

The purpose of religion is to reach the source of life, God!! God is our destination and our religion is the vehicle to get us to our destination.

Have you ever seen a person adore and worship a vehicle? Every day he'll wash, wipe, and wax that vehicle from sunup to sundown, but never go anywhere. Such individuals become so enamored of the vehicle that they forget that the purpose of the vehicle is transportation. In the realm of religion there are religious people who get so caught up in the glamour of their particular religion that they never grow spiritually. They never move from spiritual infancy to spiritual maturity. Such individuals are content to just worship their religious or denominational vehicle, but never use it to get to God.

In short, religion is the vehicle, the mode of transportation, the pipeline, the means by which we get to God (Spirituality) – the very source of life. Religion is the means by which we reach the end – Spirituality is the end. We have been religiously trained, but not spiritually educated. There is a distinct difference between training and education. Education comes from the Latin word educo which means "to bring out that which is already within," so true education is a spiritual process. It is the natural path by which we move in accord with an established pattern to manifest what we really are. The lion is called the "king of the jungle." In his natural environment of the jungle he is a very ferocious and powerful animal. There he is an educated lion – he instinctually knows how to manifest his true nature. He has been genetically coded by the Creator to function a particular way. But while all of God's creation is coded, that creation can as well be programmed to function other than God created it to function.

If we take that lion as a cub and raise him in a circus, he becomes a "trained" lion. A little puny man, with nothing but a whip and a toy wooden gun on his side makes the lion, the "king of the jungle," jump through his hoop. We all know that if that lion really knew who he was he would take the man, the hoop, the whip, and the cage and devour them all. Then the lion would run up into the stands and run you away for being foolish enough to sit watching the lion, the "king of the jungle," jump through somebody's hoop. But in the circus, he has been trained to manifest what someone else wants him to be. We have too often believed the lies that we have been told about ourselves. We must be made aware that there is something in us more precious than what others have said about us. Many of us have been "trained" to manifest other than our true nature. Oppressed, dispossessed, disinherited people, especially, have been robbed of their true identity for the sake of exploitation.

People, in general, and African Americans, in particular, have been trained to manifest other than their true nature. As it relates to African Americans, we were not allowed to be Christians, for the most part, until we had been in this country for about 225 years of physical slavery. Dr. Khalid Al Mansour notes in his book, *The Lost Books of Africa Rediscovered:* "Finally after 200 years of general neglect, the Christian leadership of America realized that the moral chaos they had constructed within the slaves had to be revised [...]."

The strategies and outlook of these Christian architects have been preserved and chronicled by the Rev. C.C. Jones in his 1842 scholarly work, *The Religious Instruction of the Negroes in the United States*. It should be recognized that far from being a racial bigot, Rev. Jones was considered an early 19th century, enlightened theologian, who wanted nothing more than to persuade America that only Christianity could constitute the emergence or perhaps, the re-emergence of a functional moral framework for the African American, both slave and free. In this proposed "religious instruction for Negroes," he insisted that everyone would be victorious – God, the slavemaster, the slave, and the country.

Rev. Jones was the advocate of a method of teaching Christianity to Negroes which became known as "oral" instructions. This method consisted of repeating questions and answers about Christianity until commitment to memory was achieved by the slaves. In teaching Black preachers and laymen he emphasized that the following must be stressed:

- God ordained slavery for the African heathen
- God ordained Whites in America to be slavemasters
- Christianity must not interfere with this divine order
- God permitted slavery in order to expose the slave to Christianity.

In pronouncing the benefits to the slavemaster for promoting Christianity to slaves, Jones said:

- The slaves will be more obedient
- Christian morality will reduce rebellions and rebelliousness, creating instead cheerful motivation, industry, domestic virtue, submission to authority, and peaceful service to the master.
- Christianity will be taught properly, that slavery is the specific embodiment of God's will and as such, should not be interfered with.

This Episcopalian preacher, who opted to explain the circumstances of the Negro based on environmental, rather than the more popular, genetic, inferiority position, also suggested that the following scriptures be used in conditioning the minds of slaves:

> "Slaves be subject to your masters [...]."(I Peter 2:18)
> "Let every man abide in the same calling wherein he was called. Art thou called being a servant...?"(I Corinthians 7:20-21)
> Paul (a Christian) sent Onesimus (a Christian slave) back to his Christian master, not to freedom. (Philemon I:10-15)

On the manner of preaching he suggested that preaching should:

- Absolutely entertain no complaints or criticisms of the slave system
- Use extensive repetition
- Use illustrated pictorial scriptures
- Have controlled integration in churches to promote subordination and inferiority in Blacks. (Usually at least two White persons had to be present when Blacks had a worship service).

Jones finally instructed slavemasters to read to slaves from John Bunyan's *Pilgrim's Progress*, and to tell them that the Bible instructs Blacks to be poor on earth; that they will get their reward in heaven.

Edward Blyden was a brilliant African American scholar, an intellectual and an educator, and an eye witness to the operation of Christianity during slavery time. In his book, *Christianity, Islam and the Negro Race,* he cites an article from *The American Newspaper* written in the late 1800s in Louisiana:

> Good teachers and preachers are very much needed in the state. I heard a preacher telling his hearers that they must go to hell, and leave their sins on the mud sills of hell before they can say that they are born again. To prove this, he said that he would quote the 53rd chapter of Isaiah. Now, what do think he quoted? Why, Bunyan's *Pilgrim's Progress*, in relation to Christians leaving the City of Destruction, and the falling off of their burdens at the foot of the cross. The mischief of the thing was that the people appeared to believe that what he was saying was really in the Bible.

Blyden further states that "the Gospel of Christ was travestied and diluted before it came [to slaves] to suit the 'peculiar institution' by which millions of human beings were converted into chattels.... The teachings they received conveyed for them no clear idea or definite impression of the religion of Christ."

Thusly, slaves and former slaves were trained to believe that it has been biblically sanctioned and divinely ordained that Blacks should be pathetic, pitiful, powerless, dependent human beings. This basic "pie in the sky" and "after a while by and by" mentality is sadly still quite pervasive in African American religious thinking.

Among all the living organisms on the earth, only the human being was created without a built-in "software" program for successful living. Insects, animals, and birds know instinctively how they must behave and what they must do in order to survive. Animals have instincts for daily living, for finding food and shelter, avoiding or overcoming enemies, and for procreation. There is a preordained pattern for all of God's lesser creatures. If this be true for animals, then surely God has a preordained plan for man, His supreme creation.

But, since man is set in a fixed environment (though he possesses abilities much more marvelous and complex than any animal) to be successful in life he needs maps and charts to guide him. He needs role models and principles or values. What then are the dynamics involved in man manifesting his true nature and purpose? What is that power or force (dynamics) that would set him in motion toward the proper development of his spiritual self?

Within Christianity we often hear phrases like "Christ is the Answer" and "Jesus is the Way." The question that must be asked is "If Jesus is the Answer, then what is the problem?" America, in general, and the African American community, in particular, are both on the brink of total destruction.

The American dream has become the American nightmare. You are not dreaming when you see that:

- African Americans own less than 1% of the private businesses in America.
- 45% of African American males from the ages of 18-29 are either in jail or under law enforcement supervision.
- Drug abuse has reached epidemic proportions.
- School dropout rates hover around 40-45% and 58% who opt to stay in school through graduation can hardly read or write.
- Crimes of violence are riddling the African American community.
- The net worth of 40% of the families in the African American community is zero or below.
- Less than 1% of the stocks and bonds owned by American individuals (not institutions) are owned by African Americans.
- The average net worth of an African American family is $3,400 compared to $39,000 for Whites.
- 30% of African American families live below the poverty line.
- Black on Black murder has reached monumental proportions.

And so when we regard the daily demise, destruction, and dissolution of the African American communities across the length and breadth of America, we face a paradoxical dilemma. The problem can best be described by recalling my days in grade school when the answers to the math problems were found in the back of the textbook. My fellow classmates knew this fact, but it was unbeknownst to me. Each day they would get perfect scores on their take-home math problems because they had simply gotten the answers from the back of the book. They did well until test time came in the classroom. Then, because they did not understand the mathematical laws, principles, theories, and dynamics to be employed in getting the answers to the problems, they failed miserably at test time.

To say "Christ is the Answer" and "Jesus is the Way" without knowing the Spiritual Dynamics to be practiced to get positive results, is to be doomed to fail miserably in the test of life. So, again, if Christ is the

Answer, then what is the problem? Christianity, in all its conventional orthodoxies, just does not meet the needs nor solve the problems of life.

Howard Thurman in his book, *Jesus and The Disinherited,* asked two foreboding questions:

1. "Is there some inherent weakness in Christianity?"
2. "Or has there been a betrayal of the genius of the Religion of Jesus?"

Jesus is the Way, but we are failing the test in our personal lives and as a community as a whole. Many of our young people have rejected Christianity as, deeming it irrelevant!

We must become attuned to the Spirit of God and let go of ideas and thoughts we know to be untrue and fruitless. We must let go of the notion of absolute reality (the idea that there is nothing else beyond physical reality).

Hebrews 11:6 reminds us that, "Without faith it is impossible to please God." Does this mean that if we don't exercise faith, God will be angry with us? No!! It simply means that just as a car operates (is fueled by gasoline), man operates properly by faith (or belief). Cars choke out without proper fuel. Man chokes out without manifesting the power of faith.

- Acts 17:28 tells us faith "gives us the power to live, to move, and be as we are."
- Galatians 5:25 tells us "if we live in the Spirit, we must walk in the Spirit."
- Romans 1:17 states "The just shall live by faith."

Just as with the grade school math books, with the answers in the back, at some juncture in our lives most of us were exposed to the Bible as the answer to all of life's problems. But no one ever told us about or gave us the formulas, the principles, the theorems to get the answers. Thus, we were left bewildered, confused and even dejected.

There is a distinct difference between a sign and a symbol. A sign offers immediate connection with the original ingredient. For example, if it has been raining outside the wet pavement connects us with the "sign" in the present, past, and the future. The wet pavement indicates that it has rained in the past, can be raining in the present, and it may rain in the future. A symbol, on the other hand, is something that represents something else much deeper and more profound in meaning. And there is no immediate connection between the symbol and what it represents.

The Bible is not God; it is a symbol of God. We have been indoctrinated to be more interested in the *miracles* of Jesus than the *mind* of Jesus. We are more interested in the *hands* of Jesus; than the *head* of Jesus; the *things* of Jesus rather than the *thinking* of Jesus; the *manifestations* of Jesus rather than the *methods* of Jesus. The fact is the head controls the hands, the method determines the manifestations. The methods, mind, thinking, and head of Jesus all represent the dynamics He employed to work miracles. "A wicked and adulterous generation seeketh after a sign, "says Jesus (Matthew 16:4).

Our problem has been that we have been intimate with the wrong things. We have been having intercourse with the results of power, but not the source of power.

Jesus, in John 14:6, declares "I am the way, the truth and the life [and] without me no one can go to the Father." Jesus is talking here about the manner, the process, and the methods He used to manifest the power He possessed. In common African American vernacular when you ask someone, "Do you know the way to make a cake?" you are asking them if they know the process or manner to be followed in making a cake. Spiritual Dynamics involves the proper methods taught by Jesus that would cause us to manifest our true nature as beings created in the image and likeness of God.

Spiritual Dynamics is not merely professing belief in God, or seeking divine assistance while remaining in a state of ignorance, impotence, and egoism. It is rather about growing and changing into our divine essence. We must learn the Spiritual Dynamics/principles that Jesus taught and practiced and employ those same principles in our own lives. If you do what Jesus did, you will have what Jesus has! This not easy, but it is possible.

Steps in Spiritual Self-Development

Chapter II

John 16:13 states "How beit when the spirit is come it will guide you into all truth..."

All of us have within us unused, untapped, latent spiritual power. I Corinthians 2:6-7 states the following:

> We do, however speak a message of wisdom among the mature but not the wisdom of this age or of the rulers of this age, who are coming to nothing. No, we speak of God's secret wisdom, a wisdom that has been hidden and that God destined for our Glory before time began (New International Version).

In other words, we were all born with wisdom that literally came out of God. Our problem is that most of us are totally ignorant of this fact.

The point here is that God has given us a secret wisdom—a wisdom to know who we are and what we were created to be. This latent unused power was in God, but when He created us out of Himself a part of it was placed in us. Now the word "secret" here does not mean to be withheld from, but it means that we have never known that it exists.

We are further told in I Corinthians 2:10 that this "hidden wisdom [is] revealed to us by His Spirit." It is the Spirit of God that allows all of the hidden power within us to become alive. God has given us the spirit so that we can understand all of the hidden power and wisdom that He has put in us.

"We have not received the Spirit of the world but the Spirit who is from God, that we may understand what God has freely given us" (I Corinthians 2:12 NIV).

The things that God has put in us are about us, who we are, what we can do, and what we can become. We are all born without a sense of self. We are like tape recorders with background music but no central theme. We are like mirrors with no reflections. First through our senses, during infancy—then through language and observation—we tape record, build, and photograph our video and audio cassettes of ourselves. For many of us this recorded self-concept or self-image is negative. Therefore, it is needless to say that much of what we have been told about ourselves must not be considered. We must forget what others have told us about who we are, and what we can do, or become. We need what is called "spiritual discernment"; the spiritual wisdom that makes possible the experience of truth.

Some things that you will come upon in reading and studying this book, you have always known to be true. Certain experiences that you have had were guided by the Spirit of God. All you need is an interpretation and an understanding of the dynamics of those spiritual experiences.

So, how do we develop ourselves spiritually? How do we know that we are growing? There are five steps we want to consider as directions for spiritual growth and development.

Step 1: The Quest

The quest involves asking the three basic spiritual questions:

1. Who am I?
2. What is my purpose in life? That is, who put me here and what am I here for?
3. What is my relationship to God and my fellowman?

These are questions some of us never get an answer to. We participate in the process of life, seeking happiness in the things of the world. Thus, our suffering is brought about by lack of knowledge (ignorance). We operate with a fundamental misconception of reality. We need a major paradigm shift.

So then, we must start with asking. Asking is crucial to learning and, thusly, knowing. It is not only crucial but, most importantly, asking is rewarding. It is the embryo of enlightenment, the germ of growth, the vitamin of vitalism and the seed of success.

Children, as soon as they are able to talk, begin to ask questions. They want to know the who, what, when, why, where and how about practically everything you show or tell them. Jesus knew that the mind works best when you ask. He said in Matthew 7:7 that the only prerequisite for being given an answer is to "ask." "Ask, and it shall be given; seek and ye shall find; knock, and it shall be opened unto you." The only requirement for discovery is to "seek," and the only condition for revelation is to "knock". There is an African proverb which states: "He who asks questions cannot avoid the answer." Do you want to have real faith or "blind faith"? That is the question. Spiritual knowledge and understanding is the only basis for real faith.

Religious "connoisseurs"—when asked questions about faith, say you have to "just believe and just have faith". As you persist on asking questions they say, "you should not question God" when you are really questioning *them*. How can you be told not to question things, when Jesus plainly says "ask and it shall be given, seek and ye shall find, and "knock and the door shall be opened?"

Dr. Francis Cress Welsing, noted African American psychiatrist, says, "If you keep your computer on, you will get a print out." All of these axiomatic expressions suggest that the mind seems to function most efficiently when we ask. A question stimulates a search for knowledge and information. The above mentioned spiritual questions all lead us on an inward journey. They are all empowering questions which direct our search toward answers which give us the power to meet a challenge, to develop toward our natural purpose, and to grow toward our fullest and greatest potential. King Solomon, reputed to be the wisest and richest man to have ever lived, asked God for wisdom. From that higher knowledge came wealth, abundance, and success.

What Moves us to Quest?

There are two basic things that cause us to begin to look for deeper meaning and purpose in life:

1. Becoming "saturated" with things so that they are no longer appealing or fulfilling.
2. Having the "things" that we have accumulated taken away from us or losing them.

Deepak Chopra, in his book, *The Seven Spiritual Laws of Success*, refers to the human preoccupation with material things as "object referral". Object referral relates to the fact that our value, our worth, or our sense of "somebodyness" is based on the status, position, property, wealth, money, cars, etc., that we have. I call them the "ego-pleasures" or "self-pleasures" of life. These ego-pleasures or object referrals are propelled by the ego which makes us have an intense need for external power. These external pleasures make us seek to control and to be approved by others. It is not too far-fetched or difficult for one to become preoccupied or even obsessed with these external modicums of success and happiness. When you don't have proper "self worth," then you seek "other worth."

Things become your sense of value, worth, meaning, and purpose. A sense of "other worth" rather than a positive sense of "self worth" evolves within the individual who adopts this false concept of self. Such ego-based power lasts only as long as that which is the object of the power lasts. Thus, if one's title, job, or money is lost, then one's power is also lost. Because the basis of power is not of the self, it is not real. Thus, when one is either stripped of ego-based power or becomes saturated or dissatisfied with this ego identity one is ready to begin to make the connection to a much greater reality. Then one becomes aware that the "ego-pleasures" of life – those things that others say give you power, just do not fulfill but leave an unseen, empty void. Such recognition uncovers the reality that we have two natures. The dilemma of an unseen part of us (that ultimately position, status, money, and things cannot satisfy) suggests that there is another part to us. We discover that the human being is more than what meets the eye; that beyond the physical self there is an unseen part of us (Spirit) which aspires to achieve greater heights than what ordinary life suggests.

Spiritual Dynamics requires us to cultivate a consciousness that leads us to the awareness of that which is beyond the realm of the ordinary – true reality. We come to understand that we, as human beings, have two natures. We are in the one instance human, earthly, fleshly, physical beings; but we are also spiritual, Godly, heavenly, divine beings. Such a revelation will ultimately put us in touch with our purpose.

Myles Monroe, in his book, *Understanding Your Potential*, states that the purpose of a thing is the "original intention" for which a thing was created. So that in order to understand our purpose, we must go back to the beginning. The word Genesis means "beginning". Genesis 1:26- 27 tells us God created us (man) in His own image and likeness, and gave him dominion over the earth. The key words in these verses are "image," "likeness," and "dominion." They are pivotal to man understanding his essence and his nature. Every product made is preceded by a purpose. "Image" does not mean a statue of something, but the very essence of the thing. When you take a picture of yourself, that is your image. It is not you, but it is a reflection of you. Sometimes when we get our pictures taken and get our proofs, we reject them saying that they do not look like us. The proofs may not look exactly like us, but they do indeed capture the essence of us.

So, to be in the image of God means that man is Godlike in character. Man, in his true nature, is not exactly like God but embodies the essence of God - His spirit. I John 4:4 states that, "[We] are of God, and greater is He that is in [us] than he that is in the world." The preposition of means "pertaining to" or "possessed of." This means that as "children of God," we pertain to God and are possessed of or have God in us. The aforementioned verse also suggests that not only is God our parent but we resemble Him so much that we have enough power to overcome anything that we will ever face in the world. The first clause of the

Lord's Prayer (Matthew 5:9) lays out the relationship between God and man as that of father and child. This clause fixes not only the nature of God, but also the nature of man. If man is the offspring of God, he must partake of the nature of God, since the nature of the offspring is invariably similar to that of its parents. It is a cosmic and divine law that like begets like. A cow does not give birth to a horse. The offspring is, and must be, of the same nature as the parent. And so, since God is God, then man must essentially be God, too; no matter how he may appear not to be. This means that man is Godlike in character, an extension of God's presence on earth. This does not mean that man is "the God", but he is "a God"—that is, God has put a part of His very self in man. Psalm 82 5-7 reads: "They know nothing, they understand nothing they walk about in darkness; all the foundations of the earth are shaken. I said, you are Gods, you are all sons of the Most High. But you will die like mere men; you will fall like every other ruler" (NIV).

This Psalm explains the current predicament of the masses of oppressed people. Because we "fail to understand" our Godly nature, we will not know anything or understand anything and we will continue to die.

Likeness means to "operate" or "function" in the way or manner of God. How does God operate? James Weldon Johnson, that great African American poet, most aptly and eruditely reflects the teachings of the Genesis story when he says after God created everything else on earth, God went into deep thought. Johnson says "God thought and thought and thought, until he thought, 'I'll make me a Man.'" Thus, God's power was made manifest through His mind. There was a process and the process started with God. Genesis 1:1 tells us "In the beginning was God." This means that before there was a beginning there was God. This means that everything that is was in God. God spoke into existence everything that there is. Speaking then must be a very powerful thing. (In later chapters we will discuss this idea in greater detail.) It will suffice to say at this point, that God (Spirit) had a thought that evolved into an attitude (decision) and then God spoke into existence all of creation.

If Man is to function or operate like God, Man must use his mind. Thus, the essence of Man is mind and that mind possesses the same quality of power as the mind of God. That is, Man has the ability to use his mind to create, develop and produce whatever he needs to, just like his Father God.

If Man is in the image and likeness of God, then to better understand Man's true nature, we need to understand God's nature. And, when we talk about God's nature, we usually refer to three major attributes – God's omnipotence (always full of potential power), His omniscience (always able to know) and His Omnipresence (always able to be). God is Supreme over all of His creation.

But, Man is in the image and likeness of God and put here to exercise "Dominion" (Lordship, Rulership) over the earth. The word "dominion:" means that man was given the position of Lord or Supreme Being of all creation. Another name for Supreme Being is God. Man is God of the earth!! Man is a son or daughter of God with all of the characteristics of power of the Father. Man as Lord of creation can manifest the same quality of power as God. Man's main purpose is to reflect God, to manifest the power of God on earth. Man was put on earth to dominate, rule, control, and direct everything on the earth.

Monroe reminds us that whatever God created, God spoke to the source of that creation. So, when God wanted plants, He spoke to the earth. Therefore, if you break down a plant botanically, you will find that the plant has the same components and essence as that of the soil. The plant is made of 100 percent dirt or 100 percent of whatever dirt is composed of. So if a plant dies and afterward lies on the ground for a period of time, it will not remain in the same state, but will once again return to the character of its original source, the earth. Likewise, God spoke to the water when He created the fish. So if fish die in your aquarium and are not taken out, the fish will disintegrate back to the character of its original source, the water. So when God wanted plants, He spoke to the dirt—when God wanted fish, He spoke to the water—but, when God created human beings, He spoke to Himself. Therefore Man is of the same essence as God, Spirit!

The Anatomy of Man

God created man in two aspects or stages. Again, James Weldon Johnson poetically reminds us that in Genesis, God first scooped dirt from the earth and shaped man out of the dust of the earth. This, however, was only part of man's creation - **Step 1.** Man was not complete. God then breathed into man the "breath of life" (Spirit) (Gensis 2:7). The word <u>human</u> is made up of two words: "humus" and "man". <u>Humus</u> means "dirt" and <u>man</u> means "Spirit". So, a human is Spirit enveloped or wrapped up in dirt. Therefore, because Spirit is the essence of God and that essence (God's Spirit) is invincible, indestructible and eternal, then we conclude in Step One that Man's primal or main essence is a spiritual one. Man came out of God (Spirit) and was given a temporary covering (a dirt body). Having made this discovery we are ready for step two.

Step 2: Identify A Source of Reference

We are now no longer bound by a limited definition of ourselves. We now know that we are not just physical, earthly, fleshly, human beings – but that we also have a cosmic identity. We are created from the same matter as the earth, the sun, the stars, and the moon. Genesis 1:1 states that, "In the beginning was God" and God then created everything else.

Modern (quantum) physics is discovering that what we seem to perceive to be is, in reality, only different aspects of the same substance. That is, when energy "vibrates" at a high speed (frequency), it appears as a light (less dense, less weight) material such as gas or electricity. The higher the vibrations are, the more subtle the "material" will appear to be. When it "vibrates" at a lower speed, it appears as a solid (dense material) object such as rocks or metals. When energy vibrates at very high rates, it goes beyond the gas state; then it appears as rays, such as sunrays or x-rays. At the highest rate of vibration, energy would be so subtle in mass that it could fit in between the "empty spaces" of the slower vibrating matter. It could pass through it or reside in it. This is the subtle realm of the "Spirit" body, which inhabits the "physical" body.

The object of all spiritual quests is to identify one's consciousness, one's concept of who one is with the "subtlest reality (Spirit)" rather than the "gross physical reality" because the physical one is perishable and transient; while the subtlest (spiritual) is transcendental or immortal. Albert Einstein started a new physics that espouses that matter, that is, everything which can be perceived with our senses including our bodies, is an "illusion." Everything (all matter) is composed of the same stuff, and the different objects we see in the world are just different combinations of the same material common to all things. Therefore even the most solid looking objects are, in reality, energy in motion at different rates of vibration.

Further, modern science has discovered that even objects of the world which appear to be separate, such as human beings, are in reality "exchanging pieces of each other" on a continuous basis. That is to say, every time we breathe out we are expelling atoms and molecules from our internal organs. Therefore every time we breathe, we are sharing pieces of our bodies with other people and with the environment. For example, air that is breathed by someone in Africa may be breathed by someone in the United States two days later, and vice versa. Thus, the physical world, which appears to have defined boundaries, is only an illusion. In reality, the world is then one interrelated mass (Genesis 1:1) of energy which is being "caused" to move and interact by some "unknown" force.

George Washington Carver, the great African American scientist and inventor, was so successful because of this understanding. He called it "relational understanding." Carver said nature is the window to God's creation. He believed that each part of the created world was connected to all others and that everything God made had a message. Carver also believed that people learned best by beginning with something they already knew, then proceeding to the nearest related unknown. Addressing "those who have not yet learned the secret of true happiness, the joy of coming into the closest relationship with the Maker and Preserver of all things," he gave this advice: "Begin now to study the little things in your home or yard, going from the known to the nearest related unknown, for indeed, each new truth brings one nearer to God." He said, "education is understanding relations."

John Ferrell referenced an article published in a Baptist periodical, in which a writer asked, "What, Dr. Carver, is the most marvelous fact of the age, or of the ages, the most wonderful conception of your mind?" Carver's answer, said the writer, was "immediate and like a flash":

> The creation story, the creation of the world. "In the beginning God... created the heavens and the earth... and God said, 'Behold, I have given you every herb yielding seed, which is upon the face of all the earth, and every tree, in which is the fruit of every tree yielding seed, to you it shall be for food[...].'" Behold means "look," "search," "find out"[...]. That to me, is the most wonderful thing of life.

Carver went on to say:

> To me, Nature in its varied forms, is the little windows through which God permits me to commune with Him, and to see much of His glory, by simply lifting the curtain and looking in.
>
> I love to think of Nature as wireless telegraph stations through which God speaks to us every day, every hour, and every moment of our lives.

He concluded that plants and animals, mankind included, are inextricably interdependent, and that the whole of creation is related to its Creator. Put another way, God is both panentheistic (God is *in* everything) and pantheistic (God *is* everything).

The Bible, Our Source of Reference

How then do we discover the spiritual principles that will foster the development of our new found cosmic identity? Where do we get information about how to develop our new found cosmic consciousness? We must identify a source of reference. We must explore the experiences of persons who developed their cosmic consciousness.

For us, as Christians, that source of reference is the Bible. Why the Bible? The Bible is used because it records the experiences of individuals who employed certain Spiritual Dynamics to attain awareness of the spiritual laws of God that govern God's creation. Thus, the goal in using the Bible as a source of reference is to extract from it the Spiritual Dynamics (principles) that made the personalities of the scriptures who they were. We must be able to put on our "Spiritual scuba diver suits," go down into the depths where they were, see what they saw, and then employ the very same principles in our lives that they did.

A good analogy to make this point clear to you would be for you to imagine yourself planning to open a food supermarket. It would be bad business sense and lack of wisdom to attempt to open such a store without consulting the management of such stores already in operation. They have already successfully done what you want to do. However, just knowing their names and titles would not help you. There would be little expected success in just lauding or worshipping what they have done. What you would rather want to do is to imitate and emulate the dynamics, the strategies and procedures and "set up" your supermarket using the same principles that they used to become successful operators. In looking at the Bible as a source of reference, our goal is to engage in bibliology, or the study of the Bible as opposed to bibliolatry, the worship of the Bible. The suffix ology means "study," while the suffix olatry means "worship." If we put the prefix "zoo" in front of the suffix "ology" we get the word zoology, which means "the study of animals." If we put the word "idol" in front of the suffix "olatry" we get the word idolatry which means "the worship of idols." We want to become bibliologists, or studiers of the Bible, rather than bibliolatrists, or worshippers of the Bible. A lot of us can recite what Paul said, what Ezekiel saw, and what Daniel felt, and yet know nothing of the Spiritual Dynamics they practiced to make them who they were.

Too many Christians *worship* the Bible rather than *study* the Bible. II Corinthians 3:6 states that, "the letter (the written scriptures) killeth, but the spirit (the dynamism in the scriptures) gives life." We must not worship the book!! At some point in our lives, probably even before school age, we were presented with a Bible and told – "This is the word of God!!" And there is a very thin line between viewing the Bible as the word of God and viewing the Bible as God. The Bible is a symbol of God, not God. A symbol is something that stands for something else, or represents something else much deeper in meaning and significance. This makes a symbol, potentially, a very dangerous thing. Without continuing to beg the point, it will suffice to say that our understanding of the nature and purpose of the Bible has been severely warped. The words "Holy Bible" are translated from the Greek words Helio Biblos. Helios means "sun" and Biblos is derived from the Egyptian word for papyrus which means "paper." Holy Bible then means "Sun Book."

Tony Browder, in his book, *From the Browder File*, states that:

> The one reality that must be faced, no matter what version of the Bible you presently read, is that the stories in the Bible are stories about African people. Over 70 references to Egypt and Ethiopia are mentioned in the Bible, more than any other nation. Much of what was written about Christianity originated in Africa because Europe, as we know it now, did not exist during that time. The story of Jesus Christ is the story of conflict and rebellion against the invading forces of the Roman armies. This story is the history of oppression against people of "color".

The invading Romans took over the African-originated religion of Christianity in the fourth century AD, led by the Roman Emperor Constantine. In AD 322 at the Council of Nicea, Constantine made Christianity the official state religion and abolished all competing religious ideology. After this conference European images replaced the African images of the Madonna and Child.

In the sixth century AD the Emperor Justinian issued an edict abolishing the last vestiges of the African religious systems. The Europeans then erected statues of the "new" Madonna and Child. Through many religious crusades, attempts were made to impose this newly created Eurocentric religious ideology throughout the world.

These undeniable historical realities help to explain the existence of over 125 versions of the "Holy Bible". The word version is from the

Latin words, *vertere* or *versum* which means "to turn or to change".

Thus despite the fact that by both name and content the Bible has an African origin, we have been given an English or Europeanized version of the Bible. Throughout the sojourn of African Americans in America, after being allowed to become Christians around 1842, we, for the most part, have been exposed to and urged to read the King James Version (KJV) of the Bible as the "infallible," "indisputable," "unadulterated," word of God. In other words, we have been given the impression that the King James Version of the Bible is errorless, has not been tampered with, and is the authentic true word of God straight from the mouth of God. The fact is, the King James Version of the Bible is not straight from heaven, not errorless, and is subject in certain instances to dispute.

This "Authorized" King James Version of the Bible was first published in AD 1611 and was necessitated by the separation of the Church of England from the Vatican. It was during a time when the reading and use of the Bible was restricted to a select few. No common folk (laborers, servants, apprentices or journeymen) were allowed to read or use any part of the Bible without risking the pain of fines, imprisonment, or even death.

The first English translation of the Bible was done by a commoner named William Tyndale in AD 1525. He went blind while translating it because he did so with little light for fear of being discovered and severely punished.

A *version*, again, is "an account from a particular point of view." For example, if ten persons saw the same car accident we might get ten different versions of who was at fault. Each person might see a different car as the cause of the accident.

We have been deceived and lied to so much, that we can see a lie and call it the truth or see the truth and not even recognize it when we see it.

On the "fly" or "title" page of the King James Version there is prima facie evidence that the King James Version of the Bible is not "unadulterated" and thus not "error proof."

The fly page reads: *"The Holy Bible containing the Old and New Testaments translated out of the original tongues and with the former translations diligently compared and revised."*

We are told first that the King James Version is "translated." To translate means to change from one language to another. And it was translated out of "original tongues." This tells us firstly, that English was not the original language the Bible was written in. Now we know that from one language to another a word can have a totally different meaning, which can totally alter the meaning of a phrase. For example, in the New Testament, the Greek word repent means literally "to have a change of mind." While in English, the meaning is to "show remorse and ask forgiveness." Then we are told on the fly page that the King James Version has been "diligently compared and revised." The word diligent means "rigorous, constant, steady effort to accomplish what is undertaken." So, the fly page relates to us that even if the original languages were used for translations, those translations were then rigorously "revised". The word revised means "to make corrections, change or amend." And, mind you, not slightly, but "diligently."

Now, the question becomes who revised the Bible into the King James Version and for what reason? History informs us that its creation was necessitated in 1534, after King Henry VIII and the Church of England separated from the Vatican because of the authoritarian, autocratic, iron hand rule of the papacy. During this period in history, you may recall that there were great restrictions on who could read and use the Bible. As previously stated by act of Parliament, no common folk, apprentices, journeymen, servants or laborers were allowed to read or use any part of the Bible, without risking severe punishment and imprisonment.

In the year 1604, King James authorized about 50 scholars to write one uniform, "official" English version (point of view) of the Bible. By royal authority, the entire Church of England would be bound to this new Bible, and all other versions would be outlawed. This is why the word "official" was used. This Bible was first published in 1611, during the same period that English slave colonies were being established in America.

To emphasize the law that no other English version of the Bible could be used King James coined the words – "infallible, indisputable, unadulterated, official word of God." As we have seen, these words were not in fact true because the fly page of the King James Version tells us so. This King James Version was deemed indisputable, infallible and unadulterated, simply because King James said so!!

Tony Browder states in *The Browder File* that William Shakespeare, a great writer of that era, was one of the scholars who worked on the King James Version. Even though all the scholars were charged not to divulge their identity as collaborators on this work, Shakespeare found a devious way to get his "signature" in the book. In the 46th Psalm, the 46th word from the beginning of that Psalm is "shake" and the 46th word from the end of the Psalm is "spear," giving us the name Shakespeare. (Psalms 46:3 and 46:9) At the time of the writing of this version, Shakespeare was 46 years old! Now what alterations had to take place so that those two words could appear at the appointed places? How did they alter the meaning? And, if Shakespeare did this, what did some of the other translators change at their own personal whim?

It is beyond dispute that not only Christianity, but also Judaism and Islam all had their origins in Northeast Africa. Christianity was taken over by the Roman Emperor Constantine in AD 325. Europe then appropriated Christianity as its own at the Council of Nicea. The emperor decreed the destruction of all other philosophies, theologies, religions and doctrines. At Nicea, the doctrine of self-salvation was distorted to the degree that the masses of people were convinced that they needed a "go between" to reach God. As their minds were thus conditioned, they forgot that they were responsible for their own fate as we, too, are today. It is at this time that references to the ability of each individual to become a Christ were either deleted or misrepresented.

Nicea moved Christianity from Africa to Rome and established a line of ruling succession directly from Peter to White popes and White officials, an uninterrupted line for almost 1700 years. The Europeans made everyone of significance White except for three Blacks: one, Simon who allegedly helped Jesus carry his cross, one of the Three Wise Men who visited Jesus at birth, and an Ethiopian eunuch who converted to Christianity after talking to Phillip.

The famous artist, Michelangelo, used his family as models to paint the ceiling of the Sistine Chapel in Rome in 1508. His aunt posed for the images of Adam and Eve in the Garden of Eden which the Bible documents as originating in Africa (Genesis 2:13). His female cousin was the model for the painting of Jesus. This imagery contributed greatly to the self-negation of oppressed people and the concomitant worship of other human beings. It also helped to infuse the acceptance of slavery in the minds of the oppressed.

There is nothing about the make-up of a human being that would make him willingly submit to slavery. He must be trained. Rev. Charles C. Jones, a White slaveowner preacher, wrote in 1842 a book entitled *The Oral Religious Instruction of the Negroes In the United States*. The book taught slave masters how to teach a "customized" version of Christianity. It started, of course, with teaching them that the King James Version of the Bible was God, Himself, speaking. Three specific scriptures were listed as being significantly important to teach slaves:

1. "Servants be subject to your masters..." (Peter 2:18-25)
2. "Let every man abide in the same calling wherein he was called. Thy calling being a servant." (I Corinthian 7:20-24)
3. Paul, a Christian, sent Onesimus (a slave) back to his Christian master, not to freedom. (Philemon)

It is easy to see from this information how African Americans were conditioned to worship the Bible as God, rather than study the Bible as the word of God. Even today, most African American churches insist that their members read the KJV *only* because it is the "pure, unadulterated, untampered" version of the Bible.

How then do We Study the Bible?

Principles are rules, guidelines, precepts or laws for effectively negotiating life. Principles are not designed to be recited or memorized. The value of a principle is to practice it and get results which becomes the natural inducement to keep practicing the principle. We must extract the spiritual principles from the Bible. We must not stand in reverential awe of the personalities of the scriptures as if they had something that we cannot have. The African approach is based on the fact that within everyone are intuitive functions that can be activated by divine guidance for correct living. For example, rather than seek to emulate David, Moses, or even Jesus; we would rather seek to discover the inner shaping dynamics of these great characters' attainments and awaken them in ourselves so that we may be guided and empowered in the same manner.

The essence of God in Man (Spirit) must become educated by Spirit (God) so that the Spirit can exercise its role as the governor of one's life. The brain is to the human body what the Spirit (the Divine Spark in us) is to the Spirit of God. The brain is the control center of the body, but it must be programmed by other parts of the body to function effectively. When a baby begins to mature you begin to try to educate that baby that some things are hot, will burn you and therefore should not be touched. You tell the baby that the pot on the stove is hot. The baby totally ignores your warning concerning the pot until one day he touches it himself. Before the baby can scream, a message about the hot pot is sent to the brain in a matter of a second. Then the brain instructs the baby to remove his hand from the pot and cry. The baby screams and no longer needs to be told that a pot is hot. The brain has now been educated by the sense of touch and can now exercise its role as governor of the body and no longer does the child need to be told that the pot is hot, but the child now tells you – "pot is hot!"

I have a cousin who cannot hear and consequently does not speak, not because he does not have the ability to talk. His sense of hearing cannot program his brain so that his brain can instruct the lips, the tongue, and the mouth how to shape and form themselves to make certain sounds. If he could hear so that his hearing could program his brain he would be able to talk. Likewise must the Spirit in Man be programmed by the Spirit of God so that the divine self or the higher self can exercise control over the lower self or the human self. There is raw potential and ability, but it must be awakened, programmed. Just as the brain is the control center of the body and yet has to be programmed before it can assume its proper role, so then must our spiritual or higher self be programmed.

There is a constant war going on between our human and our divine nature. Paul says in Romans 7:15 : "For that which I do, I allow not: For what I would, that do I not; but what I hate, that I do."

Thus in order to live we must stay connected to our source, which is God. In staying connected we must develop the ability to stay focused or another way of saying it, we must learn to develop a level of detachment to physical/material reality. Alongside the need to be detached, we must also work to not become distracted. During any given day thousands of thoughts flood the mind. We must work and struggle to remain focused. Then thirdly, we must learn to accentuate the positive, which will automatically eliminate the negative. If there has been any spiritual growth in your life, you didn't grow by dwelling on the negatives in your life. A good example of the merit in accentuating the positive and how it results in growth and progress would be to observe how we successfully advance in grade school from one level to the next.

In the first grade through the sixth grade there are some students who throw spitballs. But the true goals in the first grade are to learn colors and shapes, master the alphabet, and learn to read and to count a little. If these things are accomplished, even though spitballs are being thrown, you will pass to the second grade. However if you become preoccupied with spitball throwing and you can't stop, you will not learn what is required to complete the first grade; thus you will repeat the first grade.

In the second grade through the sixth, there is still spitball throwing, but it gets less as you focus and master what is required at each level. By the time you get to the sixth grade, spitball throwing no longer exists and spitball throwing no longer poses a problem. To be troubled by spitball throwing you would have to go back down to the first five grades.

Likewise a negative habit such as substance abuse just does not exist at a certain level. When you grow to a certain level of spiritually, the air is just too rarified for such behavior to prevail. To engage in such behavior one would have to digress back to a lower level.

Step 3: Practice the Principles

Principles must be first of all practiced in a "culture" – that is, in an environment conducive to growth. God established an optimal environment for the maximization of the potential of whatever He created. The point is as Dr. Howard Thurman says in his book, *Disciplines of the Spirit* :" Life, wherever it is found, is trying to actualize its unique potential [and] the lines along which a particular form of life maintains access to its source of nourishment and vitality involve certain patterns of behavior which, when established, become descriptive of that organism's method." When the conditions are met, energy is available. When you say a person has a "green thumb" a close look will reveal that their thumb is no greener than anyone else's. They have simply met the conditions for vegetation growth – the right amount of water, light, talking to the plants and good soil. If the process is followed, growth results.

"What is true for plants and animals, seems to be true for man." The optimal environment for man is related in the story of Adam and Eve in the Garden of Eden. God set the ideal environment when He created a garden in Eden and put Adam in the garden. God created the garden, planted the garden, organized the garden and provided everything man needed to live in the garden, including faith.

Thus, God is at the center of man's ideal environment. Man cannot live outside the environment God designed for him because he needs God's presence. We need a relationship with God which strengthens our resolve to be obedient. We must stay connected. The plant, since it was created from the soil, must stay connected to the soil in order to live. If the fish decides it does not want to live in water, get you some corn meal and cooking oil because that fish will die. Man apart from his source, God, will die also.

In addition to practicing the dynamics of spiritual growth in culture – an environment conducive to growth, there must also be positive feedback or "positive reinforcement" to facilitate spiritual growth. Even as a horticulturist fences off a baby tree to protect it while it gains strength, so must we protect ourselves, during the process of spiritual growth, by limiting contact with negative people and negative situations, and by alternatively keeping company with people of raised consciousness. The spirit must be nurtured or fed. In this respect the mind is most important to the healthy welfare of our being. The mind feeds every facet of our lives with healthy inspiration and motivation, or unhealthy depression and discouragement. The mind is a mental digestive system that feeds our spiritual and physical existence. Our minds are our mental stomachs that digest whatever we mentally consume. Therefore, we must be careful about the mental food that enters our minds. We must be concerned with our "food for thought." If we want to truly measure the quality of the mental "food for thought" we have been consuming, all we need to do is look at the true quality of our lives. Healthy "food for thought" produces a healthy mind. Healthy positive thoughts and actions produce a healthy positive life. "You are what you eat." You must not eat mental junk food!! Physical junk food produces a weak and unhealthy body. Mental junk food produces a weak and unhealthy mind. If your body gets sick, it is directly due to what you are physically eating or not eating. If your mind gets sick, it is directly due to what you are mentally eating or not eating.

Finally, there must be "repetition." In God's school there is no graduation, no seniority – we are always in the process of becoming. As such, each level of spiritual growth simply qualifies us for a higher level of growth. We must repeatedly eat, digest, and regurgitate. If we follow these outlined steps we will soon begin to see growth in our spiritual selves.

Who Is Jesus?

Chapter III

"What manner of man is this?" is the question that Jesus' contemporaries asked about Him (Matthew 8:27). And it is the same question that people have been asking ever since. The Gospel of Mark speaks for them all when it opens with these words, "The beginning of the good news of Jesus Christ, the Son of God..." (Mark 1:1).

But the most serious question to be raised is whether this perception of Jesus was shared to any extent by Jesus, Himself, or if it represents just the faith of Christians living after the time of Jesus and after His resurrection. What can we say about Jesus' self-understanding?

This is the complex and endlessly debated issue about Jesus. In Mark 1:1, Mark's belief in Jesus as "Son of God" is unquestioned. The Gospels suggest that Jesus saw Himself as acting in fulfillment of scripture. But the question still remains as to what scriptural categories Jesus used to interpret His own role.

Mark 1:2 identifies Jesus as "the Christ," "the Messiah," "the Anointed One" and the New Testament, in general, claims that Jesus is the expected King, the Son of David, of whom Isaiah and other prophets spoke. (See Isaiah 9:6-7; 11:1-2). But did Jesus see Himself as such?

There are serious doubts to be raised about this. The Messianic expectations of Jesus in Jesus' day were not nearly as clear-cut as Christians, looking back from their perspective, have often supposed. Not all Jews were looking for "The Messiah" – a Savior from the family of David. Some expected such a royal Messiah. Some had other hopes.

Also, the evidence in the Gospels that Jesus saw Himself as the Messianic King is somewhat meager. Others speak of Jesus occasionally in those terms, but Jesus, Himself, seems to show little enthusiasm for the idea.

In Mark 8:29, for example, Peter confesses Jesus as Messiah but Jesus responds to his confession with no evident enthusiasm. In Mark 12:35-37, Jesus discusses with the scribes whether the Messiah is the Son of David, but makes no direct claim.

The scarcity of the Gospel's evidence for Jesus seeing Himself as the Messiah is very striking, given the importance of this categorization for the early church. The Gospels reveal that people wanted to make Jesus King (John 6:15, Matthew 21:1-9/ Mark 11:1-10/ Luke 19:28-40); but the Jesus of the Gospels rejected many of His followers' aspirations.

Though there is some ambiguity about Jesus' Messianic consciousness, there is little doubt that He spoke of Himself as "the Son of Man". The phrase "Son of Man" occurs 69 times in the Synoptic Gospels and 13 times in John. The sheer number of times it is used and the infrequent use of the expression to refer to Jesus elsewhere in the New Testament, suggests that we are hearing the authentic voice of Jesus. But what does the phrase "Son of Man" mean? It is easy for programmed and indoctrinated Christians to miss the Hebraic "Son of" idiom. In Hebrew "a son (or daughter) of" something or someone is one associated with, belonging to, or characterized by that person or thing. A "son of courage" is a brave person or a warrior (I Samuel 14:52); "sons of light and sons of darkness" are those who belong, respectively, to light or darkness; a "son of cattle" is a calf or an ox. (Genesis 18:7). "Son of man" is therefore, simply a way of referring to a man belonging to the human species. "The son of Man" means simply "the human being". Thus in Psalm 8:4 the literal translation is "what is man (Adam) that you are mindful of him, and the son of man (being Adam) that you care for him?" The meaning is "what are human beings that You are mindful of them, mortals that You care for them?" So "Son of Man" = man = human beings. When Ezekiel is addressed by God as "Son of Man"—"Son of Man, can these bones live?" (Ezekiel 37:3); he is not being given some mysterious or exalted title but is just being addressed by God as "human being."

So when Jesus in the Gospels speaks of "the Son of Man" we should understand His words in the same way. A good example is given in Mark 2:10, "that you may know that 'the son of man' (the human being) has authority on earth to forgive sins;" and in Mark 8:31 –"'the son of man' (human being) must suffer many things."

But why does Jesus speak of Himself in this way? The popular Christian assumption is that Jesus spoke of Himself as "Son of Man" to affirm his human nature. But this is just interpretation based on later Christian doctrine and controversy. It is unlikely that Jesus needed to persuade His contemporaries of His real humanity. But in the Gospels the term "son of man" is associated particularly with Jesus and the retention of the idiom in such relationship suggests that Jesus characteristically used it.

Jesus, Son of God

Traditional Christian orthodoxy is that *Jesus* is the Son of God. But the New Testament asserts that all Christians are sons of God. Romans 8:14 states, "For as many as are led by the Spirit of God, they are the sons of God." To be a son of God is to be in a special, favored relationship with God, but need not mean anything more.

But the question is: Did Jesus regard Himself as "Son of God" in any sense? John's Gospel answers that question with a resounding "Yes" and has Jesus speak constantly of Himself as God's son. But this and many of the Synoptic references to Jesus as son of God have been seen by scholars as read back into the story of Jesus on the basis of the church's post-Easter convictions.

That Jesus did see Himself as God's son is suggested by significant evidence. Jesus addressed God as Father (Abba). "Abba" was how children addressed their fathers. Jesus seemed to use the word quite frequently – in the Garden of Gethsemane (Mark 14:36) and in the Lord's Prayer (Luke 11:2). If Jesus used the term, it suggests a special consciousness of divine son-ship on his part, but not necessarily an exclusive son-ship.

It is crucial for us to understand the life and teachings of Jesus. In the New Testament Jesus makes it clear that we are to follow Him and not worship Him. In Matthew 16:24 he says, "If any man would come after me, I want him to deny himself, to take up his cross and follow me." No where in the Bible can it be shown that Jesus called for anybody to worship Him. When folks tried to worship Him, He categorically rejected it. When a certain woman came genuflecting before Him saying in Luke 11:27: "Blessed is the womb that bare thee, and the paps which thou has sucked," Jesus rebuked her saying – "Yea rather, blessed are they that hear the word of God, and keep it." When a man came to Him calling Jesus "Good Master," He again rejected the title "good" and said, "Why callest thou me good? There is none good but One, that is God" (Matthew 19:16 & 17).

Christians see Jesus as being 99% divine and only 1% human. From this conclusion most Christians have been made to believe that we can't really be like Jesus because we see ourselves as being "only human," (1% divine, 99% human). We sing songs that sound good but, in my opinion, negate the reality of who we are. One such song that comes to mind is the very popular song sung by Rev. Thomas Walker – "I'm Only Human, I'm Just A Man." The net effect of such thinking is to see Jesus as one we can neither identify with nor imitate.

Dr. C. Scott Peck in his book, *Further Along the Road Less Travelled,* gives an example of this. He says at a conference for Christian counselors, the Rev. Harvey Cox, a theologian, told the story in the Gospels where the woman with the issue of blood accosted Jesus while He was on His way to resuscitate the daughter of a wealthy Roman. The woman begs for Jesus to cure her. He does, and then goes on to the house of the Roman centurion whose daughter had died.

He says Cox, after telling the story, asked the audience of six hundred, mostly Christian professionals, with whom they identified. When he asked how many identified with the bleeding woman, about a hundred raised their hands. When he asked who identified with the curious crowd of observers, most raised their hands. But when he asked who identified with Jesus, only six people raised their hands. Out of some six hundred Christians, only six identified with Jesus. The concept of Christianity most of us have been given makes it seem arrogant and even blasphemous to identify with Jesus, when that is exactly what we are supposed to do. We are *supposed* to identify with Jesus, *act* like Jesus and *be* like Jesus. This is exactly what Jesus calls us to do, to imitate him. A disciple is one who studies his teacher and imitates his teacher until he can function like his teacher.

But when it comes to following Jesus, not only have we been taught to worship Him rather than follow Him, but it becomes very difficult to follow Jesus when a huge period in the life of Jesus is omitted from the canonized (legally accepted) Bible. From the age of 12 to age 30 there is nothing in the Bible about Jesus. In Luke 2:42, we are told that Jesus' parents took him to Jerusalem at age 12 during the feast of the Passover. Luke 3:23 reveals that the next time He is written about in the Canon, He "began to be about thirty years of age." Then the fourth chapter of Matthew begins with Jesus' baptism at age 30.

Thus the Canon the (legally accepted books of the Bible that most of us are exposed to) deals basically with what is called the "kerygmatic message"—the birth, baptism, death, burial, and resurrection of Jesus with very little accounting of Jesus' life between the ages of 12 and 30. What happened to Jesus during these 18 years between 12 and 30? If Jesus' life during the three years (ages 30-33) before the crucifixion, that are told of in the Bible, changed the world forever, what message might be in the 18 years that we do not know about?

So in talking about the life of Jesus I think that it is important that we try to find out as much as we can about the lost years. Part of the problem we face is that Jesus did not write down anything that He did or said Himself. Dr. Khalid Al Mansour reminds us in his book, *The Lost Books of Africa Rediscovered*, that, "there is no indication that Jesus authorized, approved or authenticated anything that was ever written about Him or His teachings."

Even the authenticity of the biographical Gospels of Jesus –Matthew, Mark, Luke, and John– are complicated by the fact that the earliest copies of these Gospels were written between 100-200 years after Jesus' death.

But even more important is the fact that there were considerable conflicting manuscripts written about the life and teachings of Jesus shortly after His death. Some of these documents were regarded as heretical and destroyed, while others were accepted. Still others were expurgated (excluded).

Among the early Christians were those known as Gnostics and Copts. They lived as monks and scribes debating and rewriting the prevailing beliefs regarding Jesus, His ministry and His mission. Their writings were contemporary with Jesus and therefore great credence should be given to their accuracy or at least their relevance.

Elaine Pagels in her book, *The Gnostic Gospels,* talks about Gnosticism as a threat to Orthodox Christianity's social and political goals. Pagels states that Gnosticism was unacceptable to, and considered heresy by, those who were in the process of establishing the "Orthodox Christian Church". These Gnostic Gospels were "written out" of the Christian religion. Reverend Dr. Potter in referencing "the sacred books omitted from the Bible" states that, "they used to be included between the Old and New Testaments in fine print and preachers explained that they were not 'real Bible' that is, not inspired like the rest of the books, but might be read for historical information and general edification, provided no doctrines of Christian theology were based on them; [they] came in time to connote something spurious, counterfeit, and untrustworthy."

Potter later states "lest we should undervaluate Gnosticism because its terms, symbols and vocabulary differ so from ours, it should be stated that Gnosticism was Egyptian Christianity for the two hundred years that the leaders of the new faith (Christianity) were working out its theology. It was gradually pushed out by orthodox Catholic Christianity and its books were burned."

Marimba Ani, in her book, *Yuguru – An African Centered Critique of European Cultural Thought and Behavior,* states that, "[Gnosticism] was neither politically oriented nor materialistic enough." Pagels again tells us that individuals practicing Gnosticism could be "resurrected" spiritually through spiritual illumination and intense self-knowledge. Orthodoxy opposed the Gnostic view and was threatened by it. She states that,

> the Orthodox view of Christianity serves an essentially "*political*" function... (Pagel's italics)
>
> It legitimizes the authority of certain men who claim to exercise leadership over the Churches as the successors of the Apostle Peter. From the second century, the doctrine of [Orthodox Christianity] has served to validate the apostolic succession of bishops and the basis of papal authority to this day.

The Gnostics were deemed heretical because they did not seem to be concerned with establishing an institution that would exercise total control over the masses of people. Thus, Ani notes that emphasis within Orthodox Christianity was (and is) on the acceptance of a dogma that could be the basis of socio-political structure and control.

Both Pagels and Ani put emphasis on the institutionalization of Christianity. Pagels states that (orthodox Christianity) proved critical in shaping the Christian movement into an institutional religion. According to Pagels, the Gnostics argued that "only one's own personal experience offers the ultimate criterion of truth – an idea that would not lead to the expansion of imperial domination and control."

The Gnostics' idea of, as Iylanya Vanzant calls it, "tapping the God power within" was considered heresy in the early stages of Christianity. "That heresy," says Pagels, "encourage(d) insubordination to clerical authority."

The point to be made at this juncture is that there were considerable conflicting views about the life and teachings of Jesus shortly after His death. Gnosticism is perhaps the most conflicting of all. The Gnostic scripts were found in upper (Black Egypt – Africa) in 1945. According to the French writer Doresse:

> ...many theological critics view Gnosticism as a shapeless conglomeration of different religions, [and] disparate philosophies. We may quite possibly be dealing with hasty interpretations built up by interpreters who knew all too little about religion; so that what they took to be foundational tenants were really but the glosses or commentaries of over-literary members of sects.... Must we not suspect that the... adversaries of Gnosticism who accused it of mixing its myths with Greek philosophies and the mysteries, may often have been done so by mere rhetorical artificers and with hardly any real justification?

The Gospel According to the African Gnostics

The Gospel of Barnabas

What is the Gospel of Barnabas? It is a gospel that strikes at the very heart of contemporary Christian Christology. It is therefore important to summarize contents from selected chapters of the Gospel of Barnabas as documented by Dr. Khalid Al-Mansour in his book, *The Lost Books of Africa Rediscovered:*

- In the introduction to the Gospel of Barnabas—Barnabas is identified as "Barnabas, Apostle of Jesus the Nazarene, (called Christ)...
- Chapter 8 tells us that when Herod sought to have all "man children" killed Jesus was sent to Africa (Egypt) where he lived for seven years until Herod died.
- Chapter 10 – at age 30 Jesus received a vision through which He realized His mandate to teach the commandments of God.
- Chapter 53 - Jesus condemns all who would regard Him as the exclusive "Son of God"... and having said this, Jesus smote His face with both His hands, and then smote the ground with His head. And having raised His head, He said, "Cursed be everyone who shall insert into my sayings that I am the "Son of God."
- Chapter 70 – Jesus emphatically denies any special or unique divinity. Jesus asked "And ye: what say ye that I am?" Peter answered, "Thou art Christ, Son of God." Then was Jesus angry, and with anger rebuked him saying, "Be gone and depart from me, because thou art the devil and seekest to cause me offence!" And He was fain to cast Peter away; Whereupon the eleven besought Jesus for him, who cast him not away, but again rebuked him saying, "Beware that never again thou say such words, because God would reprobate (abandon to eternal damnation) thee."

Though these early documents were African in origin, the Christian church was gradually taken over by the White Roman political structure. Doctrines designed to reinforce the "divine right of rule," the infallibility of the Pope, and the unique divinity of Jesus were seen as crucial to the organization and survival of the Roman Empire. The dissenting views of the African Gnostics and Copts were not tolerated. Massive persecutions were therefore directed against them in the name of Jesus and they were killed as heretics and their literature was destroyed. But the Egyptian (Black) Gnostics and Copts hid their most precious documents in caves, which stayed safely stowed away until discovered in 1945.

Europe, nonetheless, appropriated Christianity as its own and through the Council of Nicea in AD 325 insisted that God had established a line of ruling succession directly from Peter to White Popes and White officials, a line that has remained uninterrupted for almost 1700 years. Despite the fact that anthropologically, archaeologically, linguistically, geographically, and in terms of Mitochrondrial Anthropology (DNA), the Bible primarily is about Afro-Asiatic people – Adam and Eve and their children, Noah and his children, the 12 tribes of Israel, Moses, David, Solomon and all of the major and minor prophets are depicted as White. (See *NewsWeek* 1/11/88 *Search for Adam and Eve*).

When Constantine, an essentially politically minded ruler became emperor of Rome, he saw Christianity as the completion of the process of unification of his empire. Rome had one emperor, one law, and one citizenship and, therefore, should have one religion.

It was at the Council of Nicea in AD 325 that the emperor made Christianity the official state religion and abolished all competing religious ideology. At this conference European images replaced African images of the Madonna and Child. Also at this conference, according to Anthony Browder in his book, *The Browder File,* all original references to astrology and reincarnation were deleted from the European Helios Biblos.

At the Nicene Council the *Nicene Creed*, known to many as the *Apostles' Creed*, was established. If you have ever attended a Catholic or Methodist Church you have heard the *Apostles' Creed* which states:

> I believe in God the Father, Almighty, maker of heaven and earth, and in Jesus Christ, His son, our Lord who was conceived by the Holy Spirit, born of the Virgin Mary, suffered under Pontius Pilate, was crucified, dead and buried; the third day He arose from the dead. He ascended into heaven and sitteth on the right hand of God the Father almighty, from thence He shall come to judge the quick and dead. I believe in the Holy Spirit, the Church Universal, the Communion of the saints, the forgiveness of sins, the resurrection of the body, and the life everlasting.

This creed determined that Jesus was the exclusive and unique Son of God and that He was of the same substance as God. The term <u>Homousia</u> was introduced which declared Jesus "unity of substance" with God.

This final decision about Jesus was not made without much arguing and controversy – the biggest of which being the "Arian Controversy." The western (White) church had reached practical unanimity regarding the unity of substance between Christ and the Father. The actual controversy began in Alexandria, Egypt about AD 320 in a dispute between Arius and his Bishop Alexander. Arius was a learned preacher advanced in years and held in high repute. He taught the unity and self-contained existence of God while teaching that Jesus was a created being having a beginning while "God [was] without beginning." Christ to him, was indeed God in a certain sense but a lower God, in no way one with the Father in essence or eternity. To Arius, Christ was neither fully man nor fully God.

On the other hand, Bishop Alexander felt that Jesus was eternal, like in essence to the Father. The controversy ensued and heightened to affect all bishops and churches who sided with either Arius or Bishop Alexander. This was the situation when Constantine reached the height of his power. The quarrel threatened the unity of the church. About 300 bishops attended this First General Council of the Christian Church. The majority in attendance had no opinion and were described by an unsympathetic writer as "simpletons." Constantine, though not baptized as a member of the church, attended nonetheless.

Williston Walker relates in his book, *A History of the Christian Church*, a creed presented by Arius which was totally rejected. A creed presented by Eusebius of Caesarea, which was vague and indefinite as to the Christological controversy of who Jesus was, was amended with insertion of the expressions, "begotten, not made of one essence (homousion) with the Father" and by the specific rejection of the Arian Formulae that there was a time when He (Jesus) was not. Thusly, under the heavy-handed influence of Emperor Constantine, this Nicene Creed was adopted. The official canonized nature of Jesus as perpetuated by the church came about as the result of the political expediency of an emperor trying to unify his empire. By the sixth century AD, then Emperor Justinian had issued an edict abolishing the last vestiges of the African Temple at Philae in upper Egypt and any aspect of the African origins of Christianity.

There remains extant other writings about the years in the life of Jesus between the ages of 12 and 30. One is the *Apocryphal Bible* or the "lost" or "hidden" books of the Bible. Even before Nicea, church leaders had pretty much decided by Christian opinion which books would go into the Canon (legally accepted books). There were three basic criteria used to determine which books went into the Canon of the New Testament:

1. Authority – whether a writer had the authority to write based on position, title or status in the church.
2. Apostolic Succession – whether one could be identified as an immediate disciple of Jesus.
3. Authenticity – whether a writing was believed to be the work of an Apostle or was just a phony representation.

Two major church councils in North Africa in AD 393 and AD 397, established the Canons of the Old and New Testaments. The Apocrypha, originally included, was dropped from the Protestant Bible at the Council of Trent (1545-63) but the New Testament books remained unchanged for almost 1600 years.

The number of gospels being set at four, and only four, was very important. Ivanaeus, in his *Adversus Hareses*, said that just as there are four winds, there must be four gospels; for the Holy Spirit, the inspiration for all divine writing, is embodied in the wind. So there are only four gospels today because there are only four winds!!

Many of the accounts of the life of Jesus were rejected by the early Fathers because they were deemed to be supplementary. The Gospel of Peter, once held as highly as Matthew, Mark, Luke, and John was ultimately rejected because it differs too much from the details in the other gospels.

Still others, like the *Nag Hammadi Gnostic Gospels* document, found in upper (Black) Egypt in 1945 were rejected because they highlighted the call to follow Jesus rather than worship Him. These Gnostic Gospels reject the enforced theology of the Roman church of over 2000 years. The Gospel of Thomas, one of these documents, opens by saying "He who understands the words of Jesus will be saved." This statement is severely different from Paul's Epistles and the chosen gospels which say all you have to do to be saved is believe.

In the book by Janet Bock called *The Jesus Mystery* more light is shed on ideas about the life of Jesus. Most of us are totally consumed by the Apostle Paul's ideas about Jesus. Paul remains the primary interpreter of the gospels, and all of the letters in the Bible are in thematic agreement with his letters. This is because by the time of the Apostolic Fathers, Paul's authority was so firmly entrenched that any apostolic letters differing from his own were rejected.

Bock was aroused by her reading of the *Aquarian Gospel*, a book first published in 1911. Her appetite was whetted by this book which contained information on the life of Jesus she had never heard before. This led her to seek more information. She soon heard of a book by a Russian author, named Nicolas Notovitch, which was published in 1890. In the book Notovitch tells of his travels to Tibet, now the northern most part of India. At a monastery high in the mountains there he discovered a manuscript which described the life of a saint known as *Issa* (the Buddhist equivalent of the name of Jesus).

Notovitch had a guide to translate the manuscript. His belief in the authenticity of the manuscript led him to write in his introduction of the translation, "I add that before criticizing my work, the learned societies could, without much expense, organize a scientific expedition having for its mission the study of these manuscripts on the spot, and thus verify their historical value." (*Notovitch's book was titled, the Unknown Life of Jesus Christ*).

It took 35 years for someone to take his invitation and in 1922 Swami Abhedananda went to the Himis Mountains, saw the manuscript, and wrote about it in his book of travels called *Kashmiri O. Tibbetti.* Bock then sought corroboration of Notovitch's manuscript.

One such corroboration was from the psychic and devout Baptist, Dr. Edgar Cayce, a trance medium, who for many years made thousands of verifiable diagnoses and cures for people thousands of miles away. He awakened from a trance one day to hear that he had spoken of Jesus' travels and studies in foreign lands in the East. He later became convinced it was true. Cayce stated that "Jesus' studies in India, Persia, and Egypt covered much greater periods then generally known or believed."

It seems impossible that the missing years of Jesus' life were so unimportant that they were dismissed and deleted. Someone obviously, for some reason, had deleted this major part of Jesus' life from the Bible. By examining the historical data of the early Christian church, it is quite evident that early church councils, especially the Council of Nicea in AD 325, changed many points of doctrine and it was possible that those missing years were expunged then because they did not coincide with the political aspirations of Emperor Constantine.

The object of relating this information is to decipher the Spiritual Dynamics at work in the life of Jesus and then put them into practice.

What did the Legend of Issa relate?

1. The manuscripts relate that, according to accounts given by merchants arriving from Judea in the same year when the

> death of Jesus occurred, that a just man by the name of Issa, an Israelite, in spite of his being acquitted twice by the judges as being a man of God, was nevertheless put to death by the order of the Pagan Governor Pilate, who feared that he might take advantage of his great popularity to re-establish the Kingdom of Israel and expel from the country its conquerors.

2. He preached everywhere the supreme perfection attainable by man.

The Bible tells of an incident in the temple, after slipping away from his parents, the 12 year-old Jesus is quoted as saying to his worried mother, Mary, "How is it that you sought me? Know ye not that I must be about my Father's business?" What was this "business"? The legend says:

> Then Issa secretly absented himself from his father's house; left Jerusalem and, in a train of merchants journeyed toward Sindh, (the ancient name for India) with the object of perfecting himself in the knowledge of the Word of God and the study of the laws of the Buddhas (Enlightened Ones).

In Bock's eventual travels to India, she met with a follower of Swami Abhedananda who in 1922 had seen the manuscripts from which Notovitch had made his copies and subsequent translations. In speaking with Swami Prajnananda, Prajnananda confirmed that his guru Swami Abhedananda had indeed gone to Tibet in 1922, found the scrolls, translated them and narrated all the incidents in the life of Jesus in his book, *Kashmiri O Tibetti*.

The legend also states that Jesus wandered about for 18 years, which corresponds with the 18 missing years in the Canon. We can glean from all of the above references that Jesus traveled extensively, and while doing so became the Christ.

Becoming the Christ

The word "Christ" is a title, not a name, just as the word "president" is a title or "king" is a title. The word Christ means the "Anointed One" or one whose head is anointed with oil. The "Anointed One" refers to any person who has manifested within his body, special talents and abilities. Throughout the ages, many persons have been given the title "Christ." The first Christ in recorded history was an African named Imhotep, who lived around 2980 BC.

Isaiah prophesied, "Unto us a child is born, unto us a Son is given." Jesus was the child and Christ was the Son. Jesus was the human, Christ was the God. (Isaiah 9:6)

In the course of Bock's research she came across an article about the lost years of Jesus by one of the great modern spiritual leaders of India, Swami Sivananda. In that writing Sivananda states that Jesus left home at 13 and returned when he was 31 years old. During his absence he traveled throughout India where he practiced Yoga. Being a perfect Yogi, Sivananda wrote that Jesus could perform miracles. He stopped the waves of the sea, gave sight to the blind, cursed lepers through his touch, and fed a multitude of people with a single loaf of bread. He further wrote that Jesus' voice is the voice of God; that through Him is expressed the call of the infinite, the call of the Cosmic being to the individual, the call of God to man. He says essentially the gospel that Jesus preached is the way of denying the flesh and asserting the spirit. He says when Jesus fasted for forty days and forty nights He was perfecting his adeptness in the science of mystical meditation. This is what he meant when he said Jesus was a Yogi. Clergyman and author Reverend Dr. Charles Francis Potter states in his book, *The Lost Years of Jesus Revealed*:

> Its seems that many Hindus believe that Jesus' "Lost Years" were, partly at least, spent in India, getting much of his best teaching from the Vedas. Didn't he say, "Take my yoga upon you and learn of me for my yoga is easy"? (Both yoga and yoke are pronounced as one syllable with the final vowel silent, and both are the same word *"zeugos,"* in Greek). Jesus perfected control of the senses, restraint and regulation of the breath and inner force – so as to create a state of absolute one-pointed concentration. In this state one transcends body consciousness, is completely dead to the senses of the body and attains spiritual consciousness. This is the religion of Jesus.

The Religion about Jesus

The religion about Jesus is basically the Apostle Paul's interpretation of the gospel. The religion about Jesus has become a doctrinal bedrock for millions of Christians. It does not issue in becoming the Christ but in worshipping the Christ. European scholars and teachers have defended, culturally supported, and even institutionalized such religion. We should note that the theology most African Americans espouse has its beginnings in European theology. This theology has been accepted "whole hog" as Biblically given, undeniably true and absolutely binding. (See previous comments on the King James Version of the Bible).

There is a "supposed" deeply rooted antiquity of this Eurocentric theology and anyone who registers a fundamental difference is dismissed as irresponsibly ignorant or demonically malevolent and evil, or both. But as was stated earlier, no matter what version of the Bible you've read, the stories you read are about African people.

We, as African Americans, need to take an African-centered approach to understanding the Bible. Geneticists and paleontologists (using Mitochrondial Anthropology (DNA) – (the same process used in the O.J. Simpson murder trial) have confirmed that the original human inhabitants of the planet earth (Adam and Eve) were Africans, and that all human beings are of African descent. As the earth's earliest inhabitants, the Africans have the longest history of knowing based on experience. *(See 1/11/88 Newsweek Magazine article Search for Adam and Eve).* Therefore, Spiritual Dynamics based on dynamic encounters with ultimate reality started with our African ancestors. People of African origin are the original practitioners of Christianity.

Let us look at the African Hebrew Jesus of history. We earlier indicated that after Jesus' temple appearance at age 12, we read no more about Jesus until age 30 when he comes to be baptized by John. Baptism was a most important ritual in the Jewish faith. In baptism a transition was sought from the condition and destiny of the unrighteous to that of the righteous. The New Testament word repent literally means "to have a change of mind". In Mark 1:4 baptism demands a repentant life. It was a baptism of conversion that marked the individual's turning from sin to God, that he might from that point live in obedience to Him.

The Baptism of Jesus

The baptism of Jesus provides a major piece of evidence in the quest for ascertaining how Jesus conceived of His function. The questions to be asked at this point are: (1) Why did Jesus come to be baptized of John? (2) What significance did Jesus attach to His submission to it? No little confusion has been aroused by the attempts to answer these questions. It is very curious to me, as well, how silent many modern commentators are on these questions.

Some European-based scholars have offered some very weak, unfortunate exegeses on the subject.

Oepke, in his writings on baptism, lists four reasons for the baptism of Jesus:

1. His sinlessness was not a ready-made and fixed conviction at this early date. (In other words Oepke was saying Jesus didn't know He was without sin and that He did not need to be baptized.) God Is Omniscient —All knowing!!
2. He could not withhold Himself from John's revival movement. (Here Oepke gets more preposterous as he proffers the notion that Jesus got so excited at the dynamism of John's preaching that before He knew it, He was overwhelmed, and in the euphoria of the moment insisted on being baptized by John. God getting overwhelmed by the skill of a human?
3. His baptism was consecration as Messiah. (That is, His baptism had nothing to do with the common purpose and meaning of baptism, but was really Jesus' coronation ceremony as the Messiah.)
4. The Messianic conception in Deutero-Isaiah included the necessity of the Messiah ranging Himself with sinners, (Explanation: He just wanted to identify with sinners.)

Now in dealing with these "reasons" or should I say "excuses" for Jesus' baptism there is first of all no virtue in taking a stand with sinners. And to identify with John's movement by no means implies the necessity of his submission to John's baptizing. Thirdly, how does Jesus view as an appropriate means for Messianic consecration, a rite generally viewed as a means of acquittal? Lastly how could Jesus, presuming that He is the Lord and Savior of the Christian church, occupy such a position as a repentant sinner? The Messiah was not usually thought of as a sinner!

I contend that Jesus, like others, could bury His past beneath the waters of Jordan, and rise to a new life in accordance with God's will. Since John's baptizing was an expression of repentance and a desire for forgiveness, we need to acknowledge that Jesus knew His need for forgiveness and was baptized to receive it. Jesus, whatever else he was, was the incarnation of honesty. Jesus would never have sought baptism for the remission of sins had He not been conscious of sin.

His baptism was not, as many orthodox Eurocentric scholars propose, His first step in bearing the sins of the world. I do not believe that Jesus would participate in such a sacred and deeply profound, meaningful and important ritual to achieve a general baptism for the sins of the world.

This baptism, as for any other repentant sinner, represented a turning point in the life of Jesus. To go through the ritual of baptism suggests that His "old mind," His "old thinking" needed to be buried through the ritual of baptism. Jesus insisted on being baptized:

> Then Jesus came from Galilee to the Jordan to be baptized by him. But John protested strenuously, having in mind to prevent him, saying, "It is I who have need to be baptized by you, and do you come to me?" But Jesus replied to him, "permit it just now, for this is the fitting way for [both of] us to fulfill all rightousness–" that is, to perform completely whatever is right... (Matthew 3:13-15 Amplified Version).

Now this idea of Jesus' baptism is crucial to our following Jesus rather than worshipping Him. Jesus tells us clearly in Matthew 16:24 that if we are to be His disciples that we must follow Him. If we see Jesus as having been always totally sinless, totally perfect and then we look at our own sinful nature, we are presented with an impossibility from the very beginning. Jesus came to show us that Christ, the image of God, is in all of us! The word image means the "essence of the being." Christ is the image of God. That means when God created you, He created you in His image, and His image is Christ. When I was a child we used to play a game called "follow the leader." In the game a leader was chosen and then everybody had to do what the leader did. If the leader climbed a tree, everybody had to climb the same tree. If the leader jumped over a puddle of water, everybody had to attempt to do the same. One by one as the followers were not able to imitate what the leader had done, they dropped out and whoever was the last one left was the winner and became the new leader. How can we be Jesus' followers if we are imperfect and He was always totally perfect?

Jesus calls us to be disciples and follow Him. A disciple is a learner who follows a teacher everywhere he goes. His goal is to learn and keep learning until he resembles the teacher. The follower's greatest desire is to know and resemble the master's life. Jesus said in John 14:12, "Marvel not at the works that I do, the works that I do shall ye do also; and greater works than these shall ye do[...]."

If we are called to follow Jesus, and He was always unblemished and perfect, while we ourselves are imperfect beings, then we are presented with an impossibility from the very beginning. However, when we see Jesus as a human being who became the Christ (the very essence of God) we see the very real possibility of our being able to follow Him.

It is clear in reading the scriptures that Jesus urged loyalty to God, and not worship of Himself. This is to say that Jesus was theocentric, or God-centered. Jesus gives to us a completely different orientation than that of the Christian church. Jesus taught and practiced Spiritual Dynamics that could be practiced in every human being's life. The orthodox message of the New Testament is undeniably Christocentric, or Christ-centered. During Jesus' lifetime he was the proclaimer of God, and after His death there was a shift of focus where He became the proclaimed.

Of all the titles bestowed upon Jesus, none of them was self-applied. Jesus was not only always praying to the Father, but He was constantly pointing people to the Father. Two scriptures come to mind in describing His position:

In Matthew 19:17 – When the rich young ruler called Him "Good Master" Jesus replied, "Why callest thou me good? There is none good but one, that is God."

In Matthew 5:48 – Jesus says, "Be Ye Perfect even as the Father in Heaven is Perfect."

Why did the Proclaimer become the Proclaimed?

It was the life-saving, life-transforming, salvation experience that made people begin to worship Jesus rather than follow Him. It was the profound "big bang" experience that transformed persons lives that made people adopt a "Jesusism". The proclaimer becoming the proclaimed is based on one or the other of the following:

1. Love Language – Love is really an indefinable, inexplicable term. How does one really describe what loving someone really means to him? It is like a person saying, "My mother is the sweetest mother in the world." That person is simply trying to define what his mother means to him. How does one describe how he feels about all the things that his mother has done for him? It is indescribable and thus one uses terms that speak of his mother as being the "greatest," the "most wonderful" mother in the world.
2. Survival Language – In an effort to survive against stiff competition from other religious philosophies, and even different strains of Christianity, the early followers of Christ in the second and third centuries felt they had to make Jesus more powerful and greater that the God of any others.

A person is alright in making such a statement until he tries try to convince another person who has a mother who he, too, feels is the sweetest mother in the world.

The Apostle Paul's favorite way to describe Jesus was "the Lord." Kyrios, 'Lord' was used in a wide range of contexts. It was used by the masters of slaves (as in Colossians 4:1, Ephesians 6:9, and in referring to Greek deities I Corinthians 8:5-6) and by the Jews in speaking of Yahweh.

For Paul, the word Lord had two major connotations. First, it was a word through which Paul could express what his experience of and relationship with Jesus had done for him. He saw himself after his conversion as the "slave" or "servant" of Jesus "the master" (Romans 1:1). Lord to him, suggested one who gives instructions and one who is to be obeyed.

But Paul did not see Jesus as just a human master. He saw Jesus as divine. The second way to use the word Kyrios 'Lord' was to express this conviction. He tries to describe the "indescribable" by calling Jesus "Lord." One of the striking features of Paul's letters is that from time to time he applies Old Testament statements about Yahweh to Jesus. Thus in Romans 10:13 Paul uses the promise of Joel 2:32 that "everyone who calls on the name of the Lord shall be saved." He echoes the words of Isaiah 45:23 about knees bowing to Yahweh, when he speaks of "every knee bowing to the exalted Christ." The word "Lord" was clearly extremely important to Paul and made Jesus one to be "Proclaimed," though Jesus, Himself, was the proclaimer of the Father God.

It is clear that the titles and proclamations about Jesus have their origin in the saving experience of individuals and the community of believers. Such a saving experience by Jesus was an experience of revelation. Jesus made something known to them, something that not only satisfied their minds but transformed their lives. It was the sense that they found what they were looking for in Jesus that started a worship of Jesus as "Lord." One cannot have such a mind-boggling experience of the power and reality of God without proclaiming the source of the experience the "One and Only". The result is love language – a "myopic Christocentrism," a "Jesusology," a reductionism that absorbs God into Jesus. And such a Christocentrism violates not only Christian revelation but the revelation found in other faiths.

Jesus, on at least two occasions, tried to rid His disciples of the "cataracts of provincialism" but, in far too many instances, this "love language" appears to have prevailed.

Jesus and Paul: Christianity vs Paulinanity

Chapter IV

Paul – Follower of Jesus or Founder of Christianity?

Jesus and Paul are the dominant forces on the pages of the New Testament, more than any other figures. And they are quite different and distinct from each other in many ways. Jesus was a charismatic, grass-roots leader and teacher, while Paul was a Greek-speaking, educated, intellectual letter writer. It is obviously clear that both played a vital role in the establishment and the early development of Christianity.

The question to be raised as we consider the early development of the Christian movement is: What was the relationship between these two men? As far as the Canon is concerned there is no evidence that they ever met in Jesus' lifetime. We do know, however, according to the Book of Acts, that Paul came into contact with some followers of Jesus (Peter, James, John, etc.) soon after Jesus' death. Paul very fiercely opposed them at first, but after his dramatic Damascus Road conversion he joined them and became, in his own words, a "slave of Jesus Christ" (Romans 1:1). It is commonly assumed, by most Christians that Paul's relationship with Jesus was that of a faithful follower; that as a self-confessed "slave of Jesus," Paul was profoundly interested in the life and teachings of his master. Such an assumption is further extended to conclude that he based his own life and his teaching on what he knew about Jesus.

I want to suggest that such an assumption is not just untrue, but a gross misappropriation of the facts about Jesus' and Paul's relationship. Paul, far from merely following the teachings of Jesus, was an innovator who brought into Christianity all sorts of ideas and emphases that complicated and spoiled the original simple religion of Jesus. Many of the views of Christianity that are "unacceptable" and "unpleasant" to many of us came from Paul. Negative attitudes toward women, Jews, slavery, and sexuality came largely from the teachings and writings of Paul. He took the relevant simplicities of the Sermon on the Mount and upstaged them with divisive, dogmatic rigidities.

I am suggesting that there was a major divergence in the early church between the Jerusalem apostles (Jesus' disciples) and Paul. My attempt in discussing the teachings of Paul is not to impeach the unique personal credentials of Paul. However, because Paul's extension and elaboration on the teachings of Jesus constitute the essential basis of Christian dogma and doctrine today, we must revisit Paul. It is largely due to Pauline thought that the Jesus of history, the prophet of Nazareth, has become the unchallenged "Christ of Faith." The common assumption, that after Paul's conversion that Paul was a faithful follower of Jesus and deeply committed to the teachings of Jesus, is in my opinion, a very faulty supposition.

In chapter 3 we referenced the fact that the Gnostic Gospels written close to the time of Jesus' crucifixion were deleted from the Canon (the accepted or legal books of the Bible). Those Gnostic Gospels speak about the ability of each individual to become a Christ. In the *Essence of the Gospel of Peace,* translated by Edmund in the early 20th century: Jesus states His teachings are to help guide those seeking to attain "His" level of consciousness to become as He was, a Christ. Another Gnostic text, the *Gospel of Thomas*, which contains many of the sayings found in Matthew, Mark, Luke, and John states that those who "understand and follow my teachings shall be my disciples." These sayings directly reflect the teachings of Jesus.

Jewish theologian Klausner in his book, *From Jesus to Paul,* states that "little by little, the Christ of Pauline theology took over from the holy man of Galilee." Similarly, in his *Religion of Jesus* Klausner raises the question "Is it an exaggeration to suggest that oceans separate Paul's Christian Gospel from the religion of Jesus the Jew?" It is not only Jewish scholars who see Paul in this light. Other scholarly works which pose a significant gap between Jesus and Paul include Casey's *From Jewish Prophet to Gentile God* and Macks' *The Lost Gospel.* Both trace many of the central Christian *myths* to Paul. As we shall see, the orthodox Christian Church has based its doctrine and life not on Jesus, but on Paul and his misinterpretation of Jesus.

The issue is how faithful a follower of Jesus was Paul in his failure to refer much to Jesus' life or teaching. In his letters, Paul refers very frequently to the death and resurrection of Jesus, but as for Jesus' birth, baptism, miracles, parables, transfiguration, etc., there is a deafening silence. As for the sayings of Jesus, Paul hardly quoted them!! It is not just that Paul uses little or no quotations of Jesus in his teachings, but Paul fails to quote Jesus specifically when it would help him to make a point. For example, in II Corinthians Paul urges believers to be more generous in their giving. He uses many arguments to press them to respond, but does not involve the great teachings of Jesus about wealth, poverty and "laying up treasures in Heaven." Why was Paul almost totally silent about Jesus' teachings? The obvious conclusion is that Paul simply did not know. This is quite the logical conclusion. If Paul had known about Jesus' ministry and teaching and they were important to Paul (just like modern Christian preachers), he would surely have referred to them continually. The fact that he did not, points to Paul's ignorance of the teachings of Christ, or their unimportance to him.

How could Paul have been uninterested in Jesus' life and yet call himself a "slave of Jesus Christ"? Paul focused only on the death and resurrection of Jesus. It was *this* Jesus that Paul worshipped and served. What the earthly Jesus did and said was of very little importance to Paul. The influential Rudolph Bultmann says, "Jesus' teaching is, to all intents and purposes, irrelevant for Paul." We know these facts and yet there is a reluctance to openly test the implications of Paul's thinking for today's world. In the chaotic confusion of today's world, many people come to the church for resources to help them to positively bounce back from their pain. If the pain is deep enough the conventional orthodoxy of Pauline thought just does not satisfy. More often it fosters conflict, confusion, resentment and even despair.

We have to look at two very important questions:

1. Did Paul use or depend on the teachings of Jesus in developing his theology?
2. Is Paul's theology similar to or dissimilar from Jesus'?

Let us examine these questions by taking a look at the major themes of Jesus' teaching, as recorded in the Gospels, and compare Paul's teachings on the same subject. As we look at this comparison we will consider whether there is any evidence to show that Paul was either influenced by or knew the teachings of Jesus. Does Paul make any allusions to Jesus' teachings or even "echo" in deliberate and direct fashion any of the sayings of Jesus?

Two Distinctly Different Messages? Comparing Jesus and Paul

The question of Paul's knowledge of the sayings of Jesus is not the only point of discussion of Paul's relationship to Jesus. What about their message? Many take for granted that the two preached the same Gospel. But even a cursory observance will show significant differences between what Jesus and Paul preached and emphasized.

Personal Accountability (Atonement vs. Attunement)

- Jesus says in Matthew 16:24 that every follower is personally accountable and responsible; that every follower must do exactly as He (Jesus) had done. Jesus talks about personal experience.
- Paul says in Romans 10:9 that one need only verbally acknowledge Jesus as Savior and believe He was "raised from the dead and would then be saved." Paul talks about intellectual belief.

The Kingdom of God

The entire ministry of Jesus is based on the "Kingdom of God." In Mark 1:15, the ministry and message of Jesus is introduced (at least according to Mark). Matthew and Luke agree with Mark. Matthew just changes the expression from "Kingdom of God" to "Kingdom of Heaven." Matthew and Luke also agree that the "Sermon on the Mount" has to do with the Kingdom i.e. – "Blessed are the poor" for theirs is the Kingdom (Matthew 5:3; Luke 6:20). The writers of both of these gospels both agree that Jesus' disciples were sent out by Him to proclaim the Kingdom (Matthew 10:7; Luke 9:2). There is overwhelming evidence that Jesus proclaimed the coming of the Kingdom. Though biblical scholars disagree on many, many interpretations, they are practically unanimous on Jesus' focus on "The Kingdom."

But what did Jesus mean when he talked about the Kingdom and how does that jibe, if at all, with what Paul focuses on as the emphasis of his message? Here is where we begin to have a serious scholarly theological breakdown. Quite frequently the "Kingdom of God" seems best viewed in reference to the "reign" or "rule" of God.

As the term is "fleshed out" in the modern day church it has come to refer to becoming a "member of the institutional church" whose goal is to bring everyone in the world into this "physical" Kingdom of God – the institutional church where God is King over its life.

When Jesus spoke of the kingdom he told his disciples in Matthew 6:10, and in Luke 11:2 to pray for the establishment of the Kingdom. He also speaks of the Kingdom as something to be "entered" or "not entered" (Matthew 18:3, Mark 10:15). These scriptures refer to getting into the "realm" of God, which is the "Spirit realm." It does not in any sense refer to a geographical location.

To appreciate Jesus' perspective it is very helpful to be reminded of Jesus' context. Palestine had been under Roman rule since 63 BC. There was the "PAX Romana" or the "Peace of Rome" which tolerated Eastern religions so long as the practice of those religions did not interfere with the laws and regulations of the Roman government. But there were all kinds of pressure on Jesus and His fellow Jews at the time that He was living in Rome. There was severe economic trauma for a great many of the Jews living in Rome. Many suffered great hardships, losing their land, their jobs and businesses, and going into great debt.

While some Jews fared well in Rome, the disparities between the rich and the poor increased painfully. Add to this the hated Roman tax and the apparent defecting of some Jews (Pharisees) to the evil ways of the Roman oppressor, and you have the makings of a particularly traumatic environment.

In this sense, Paul and Jesus came from two totally different social environments.

Paul and Jesus had totally different upbringings. Just as it is difficult for one who has been fed with a silver spoon to understand what it means to live in poverty, facing sheer survival on a daily basis; in the same sense, we must see the difference in the environments of Paul and Jesus.

Jesus was an African Hebrew in the midst of an oppressive White Roman government. He grew up in the ghetto of Nazareth where it was asked — "Can anything good come out of Nazareth?" (John 1:46) As one in a family of at least nine members, the Gospels of Mark 6:1-5 and Matthew 13:5 tell us that he had four brothers, James, Joses, Juda, Simon, and though unnamed in the scriptures, at least two sisters. So, there were at least nine members of His family. His father was a carpenter, a job in that era, which was a hardly-can-make-ends-meet job which made it difficult for Joseph to even pay his taxes (Luke 2:5). **Paul, on the other hand, though a Jew, was deeply schooled in Greek philosophy and law at the feet of Gamaliel in Jerusalem**. He had become a "Hellenized" Jew acculturated in Greek culture and thought.

Jesus was poor! In the second chapter of Luke when Jesus' parents took him to the temple to dedicate him back to God, they used turtles and doves for their sacrifice. The law of Leviticus stated that "when the days of her purifying are fulfilled, for a son... she shall bring a lamb of the first year for a burnt offering. And if she be not able to bring a lamb, then she shall bring two turtles or two young pigeons" (Lev. 12:7-8). From the text of Luke it is clear that Jesus' mother could not afford to sacrifice a lamb, so she used doves or young pigeons (Luke 1:23-24). Thus, the economic predicament with which Jesus was identified at birth, placed him, says Howard Thurman, "initially with the mass of poor people on the earth."

Paul, on the other hand, though by blood, training, background and religion was a Jew, he was a free Jew and was a citizen of Rome. There is a very wide gap between his status in the Roman Empire and Jesus'. He had citizenship rights, Jesus and the majority of His fellow Jews did not. **Paul was a minority but with majority privileges.** Paul had guaranteed rights and it is then quite understandable that his sense of security would influence certain aspects of his philosophy of history. Naturally, he would have respect and regard for the government and the governing laws of Rome. It is not surprising then to hear him tell slaves to "obey [their] masters like Christ", and say "all government is ordained of God" (Romans 13:1). This teaching was used, and continues to be used, to keep African Americans and other minorities oppressed and in slavery. Oppressed people were taught to submit to wicked, oppressive rule because they were taught that that rule was sanctioned by God. The point to be emphasized here is that this aspect of Paul's teaching is understandable when we consider his Roman citizenship. **Jesus, on the other hand, was much more a member of a minority group in the midst of a larger dominant group.** The masses of African Hebrews had lost their status when in 63 BC Palestine was conquered and controlled by Rome.

Jesus was Black. The genealogy of Matthew tells us in Matthew 1:3,6 that two of Jesus' ancestors were Hittites, who were descendants of Canaanites, who were descendants of Black Ham. In Matthew, the second chapter, when Herod decreed that all African Hebrew boys should be killed, Jesus' parents took him down into Egypt, the land of the Blacks, to hide. No blue-eyed, blonde-haired Caucasian could have hidden out in Black Egypt. Tacitus, the Roman historian of antiquity in AD 70 tells us that the original Hebrews were African and Arthur Koestler, a European Jew, tells us in his book, *The Thirteenth Tribe,* that European Jews converted to Judaism. He admits that the subject matter produced mixed feelings within himself. As a self-professing Jew, he did not want to be seen as betraying his people. But as a committed intellectual he had an uncompromising, scholarly commitment to search for truth. He thusly tells how a relatively small number of Russians in the eighth century

(AD 740) were able to penetrate the previously Middle Eastern religion of Judaism through conversion.

The historical setting in which Jesus grew up, the economic and social predicament, his minority status, and his blackness are all important. As well, any explanation of Jesus in terms of politics, economics, social status and mentality would also describe the masses of His contemporaries. It is absolutely beyond reason to assume that the agonizing problems facing Jesus' people did not concern Him, or that He did not develop a definite attitude and position about the plight of His people. The critical question He and His fellow oppressed people faced is, says Thurman, "How do we overcome? How do we survive as an autonomous, cultural, religious and political unit in the midst of a hostile Hellenistic world?" In the face of such persistent disrespect and injustice, Jesus' message focused on a radical change in the inner attitude of the people. He offered an inner attitude for dealing with the oppression of Rome. Rome was the enemy and Rome symbolized frustration and fear.

Jesus faced the same situation oppressed people face today. What must be the attitude or response toward the rulers, the controllers of political, social, and economic life? Jesus' response was expressed in this brief statement - "Know ye not that The Kingdom of God resides in You?" (Luke 17:21) Howard Thurman states, and I concur, that Christianity as borne in the mind of Jesus was a strategy of survival for the oppressed. The fact that it ultimately became the religion of the powerful and dominant, used as an instrument of oppression, must not tempt us to believe that this was the idea in the mind and life of Jesus. Many today find little relevance in the orthodox teachings of the Church about Jesus. It is, to a large degree, seen as a euphemism of White racism - a betrayal of the masses into the hands of the enemy by focusing on heaven, forgiveness, and love for everybody.

Many of Jesus' oppressed contemporaries looked to Jesus for a military and political revolution and His followers hoped that He was about to take power, perhaps even by force, and that they would subsequently enjoy new and privileged positions in this new order. Luke tells us in Luke19:11 that they supposed that The Kingdom of God was to appear "immediately!!"

But Jesus clearly did not see the Kingdom in those terms. Jesus' understanding of the Kingdom was "Spiritual" rather than political or material. The gospels associated Jesus' healings and exorcisms, His concern for sinners and empathic identification with "outsiders" and the "poor" with the coming of the Kingdom. In Jesus' parable of the lost sheep in Matthew 18:10-14; and in Luke 15:3-7, His mixing with tax collectors and "undesirables" is consistent with His idea of the Kingdom as a time of restoration of the satanic, the sick and forgotten, all of whom were in need of being brought back into the "Kingdom" (under the rule of God) and not under the oppressor.

Thus Jesus' view of the "Kingdom" was based on social liberation and reconciliation.

Jesus had a view unlike His contemporaries about how to bring about this social liberation and reconciliation. He saw the human problem as having inner implications, as a matter of the "heart." In the seventh chapter of Mark, Jesus criticizes those who had a preoccupation with outward cleansing when He explains that "it is what comes out of a person that defiles" (Mark 7:20-21).

Now if Jesus' assessment of the human problem was in terms of the "heart," then He saw the coming of the Kingdom as the solution to the problem that would transform the individual from within. Jesus not only diagnoses the human condition, but He also offers a solution, and that solution is in terms of inner renewal.

Now, let us observe briefly Paul's teachings. We have already stated that the Kingdom for Jesus was "the good news." In Mark 1:15 where the heart of Jesus' message is identified as the Kingdom, Mark states, "the time is fulfilled, and the Kingdom of God has come near; repent and believe in the good news."

For Paul, the good news is about Jesus. In Romans 1:1-4 He speaks of "the gospel of God, (which he promised beforehand through his prophets in the holy scriptures) concerning his Son, who was descended from David according to the flesh and was declared to be the Son of God with power, according to the spirit of the holiness by resurrection from the dead, Jesus Christ our Lord."

The centrality of Paul's message is what, in theological circles, is described as the "kerygmatic message" – the death, burial, and resurrection of Jesus. This focus on Jesus is divergent from and opposite of Jesus.

Thus, Paul's gospel is the "religion about Jesus" and is thusly different from the "religion of Jesus" (what Jesus taught and practiced). Paul's interpretive transformation is what gives us the "religion about Jesus."

Another major divergence between the teachings of Jesus and the writings of Paul is Paul's "substitutionary theory" which opposes

Jesus' idea of the need to imitate and follow Him. Paul says in Romans 10:9 that Jesus has already done everything through his death and resurrection and we need only to accept that He has done so by simply saying, "I believe." Jesus, on the other hand, says in Matthew 16:24 that if we are to be His followers, we must deny ourselves, take up our cross and follow Him!!

For Paul, there is a "justification" or acquittal of individual sinners by God on the basis of what Jesus has already done for us. It cannot be doubted that this "justification" is a central Pauline theme. Such an idea is no where apparent in the teachings of Jesus.

Equally, **Paul talks more about "faith" as an intellectual belief versus the idea propounded by Jesus that we must have a "personal experience" with God which actualizes our faith**. Thus Paul can say, "If you confess with your lips that Jesus is Lord and believe in your heart that God raised Him from the dead, you will be saved." Jesus comparatively says that every believer is personally accountable and responsible. Every follower must seek then to imitate Jesus.

We can therefore conclude that the true teachings of Jesus have been obscured by the easy, neat, systematized closed theology of Paul, which is neither life-changing nor empowering. The Christian life, as explained by Paul, does not consist of developing the individual personality, improving society, or in making the world a better place in which to live. **Paul promotes absolution of both accountability and self-responsibility. On the other hand, the teachings of Jesus require,** according to Dr. Leon Wright, in his book, *From Cult to Cosmos: Can Jesus Be Saved?* **"a continually embattled quest for meaning and purpose, which leads to an emboldened, enlightened, empowered existence.** Hence, the injunction of Jesus to 'seek,' 'knock,' 'ask' with all your heart."

In Paul's own words he said:

> For I would have you know brethren, that the gospel which was preached by me is not according to man. For I neither received it from man, nor was I taught it, but received it through the revelation of Jesus Christ... Neither went I up to Jerusalem to them which were Apostles before me; but I went into Arabia, and returned again to Damascus (Galatians 1:11,12,17).

Now the fact is that Paul, before developing his own theology, never met Jesus nor did he consult with those (Jesus' disciples) who had been exposed directly to Jesus' teachings and His work. Paul never met Jesus in the flesh. And when he became converted (Galatians 1:16&17) he did not consult with Jesus' disciples who had walked and talked with Jesus, but rather went to Arabia (Africa) and developed his own theology. Paul limits our access to Jesus and thusly robs us of the power of God available to us. The perpetuation of the "Biblical mystery" introduced by Paul has now been institutionalized, socialized and glorified. The Canon has imposed "strict theological limits" which are difficult to rise above.

What do we do with Paul?

Am I suggesting that we repudiate or reject the teachings of Paul? The answer is an emphatic "NO!!" But, we must build on Paul's visions. We must revisit Paul's interpretation of Jesus!! If you are a bibliolatrist, this will frighten you. If you desire to truly follow Jesus, it will ultimately enlighten you. We must recover the Spiritual (Cosmic) Dynamics of the African Hebrew, Jesus the Christ. We must, armed with such a cosmic awareness, search out a contemporary understanding of life that Paul's kerygmatic teaching has served to limit. We must reconsider the man, Jesus. The quest for the historical Jesus leads us to cosmic groundbreaking experiences regarding the nature and destiny of man. We have relied too heavily on the notion of Jesus as "Lord" at the cost of pregnant possibilities within our nature as beings in the image and likeness of God.

All of us can be "Son of Man" and "Son of God." Paul knows no more about God than we can know. God is not dead; if God is not dead, then He is still speaking and still revealing Himself. We have been trained and purposely conditioned to nostalgically live in the past under the protection of passionate, partisan, dogmatic propaganda. All of us must have a "personal encounter" of our own with God to understand the actualities people in another time (the Bible) referred to. We must go back to Jesus!! If we do what Jesus did, we will have what He has!! (John 14:12). We need information about ourselves and the wider reality of which we are a part. As long as we allow European Christian "scho(liars)" to insist upon locking all truth within biblical confines, we will learn little of the personal, mystical power that Jesus taught about.

The ultimate criterion of the scrupulous, conservative guarding of Pauline thought is the difference it makes or fails to make in the quality of being. In the dictums of Paul, people have not become observably better from one generation to the next. Racism is not better, in fact it is worse. Poverty is not being overcome. Today's public policy has its roots in the same soil of parochial alienation as the hostilities by Christians during slavery. The dogma and doctrine of Paul have been allowed to supply both the content and potential of Christian experience. Within orthodox Pauline thought, there is no goal except to sit down and be saved.

The principle emphasis of Jesus' ministry was an "ethical, works related thrust" which has been historically muted in favor of sacramental concessions to "human frailty." We must understand and remember that the church's dogmatic posture of "Jesusism" grew out of the dynamics of first century insecurities and values. Jesus pointed the way for a universally applicable spiritual direction for man. Jesus moved (evolved) from Jesus of Nazareth to Jesus, the God-man. The divine credentials of Jesus have been embellished to the exclusion of the exceptional "Jesus, the man."

Paul speaks in Romans 1:3 of Jesus as God's son "who was descended from David according to the flesh." Please note for future reference that when Paul uses the word flesh, he does so to refer to the sinful human nature in contrast to the life of the Holy Spirit. Thus in his mini-history of Jesus in this first chapter of Romans, Paul speaks of Jesus in His fleshly weakness and then on His Spiritual life of resurrection power. In Galatians 4:4, Paul speaks of Jesus being "born of a woman." All of this is very important when we review Jesus' mandates to follow Him.

In several passages Paul speaks of Jesus directly or indirectly as "the new Adam." "Adam," being a great figure in Jewish thought, is the archetypal and original human being (Romans 5:12).

In Phillipians 2:7 where Paul speaks of Jesus in human likeness and form, he does not mean that Jesus only seemed to be human, but rather that He exchanged the divine form for the human form. Similarly in Romans 8:3, Paul speaks of Jesus being sent "in the likeness of sinful flesh." Paul sees Jesus as the new and greater man who was in the image of God and who brings restoration of the image to others. In this respect he would be in agreement with how Jesus saw Himself. Paul believes in Jesus' real humanity. He speaks in Galatians 4:4 of Jesus being sent by God and being "born of a woman, born under the law".

As we move from the picture in the Gospels of Jesus – a poor, economically deprived child from the ghetto of Nazareth to Paul's picture of Jesus— the risen Christ, this is not an exaggerated difference. Paul saw Jesus primarily as a divine figure while Jesus saw Himself as the highest expression of what man in the image of God is supposed to look like.

Some of the differences can be explained in terms of their differing contexts. But much of it is explained in the fact that Paul never met Jesus in the flesh (at least according to Canonical writings) and was never exposed directly to Jesus' teachings and thusly made his own interpretations of Jesus' message. In the words of Bultmann, Paul greatly fostered the transformation of Jesus the "proclaimer becoming the proclaimed" where instead of teaching believers to "follow Jesus," he rather taught them to "worship Jesus."

Vod Twum–Barima, Ghanaian metaphysicist and student of the ancient esoteric sciences, in his book, *Man Know Thyself,* says that "the Delphic Oracle by the same name was a divine injunction to understand the special relationship between man and the universe [God]; the Great Architect." He further states that this teaching originally came out of the Ancient Mystery Schools of Egypt where on the walls of those schools was inscribed the words "Man Know Thyself."

There were special teachings given leading to the tapping of the divine power within. This knowledge of the "Kingdom of God," as it was then known, revealed the secrets of nature – physical, psychic, mental, and spiritual – which helped to develop the hidden powers of man.

The Frenchman, Robert Charroux, in his book, *The Mysterious Unknown,* discusses the power of those who entered the Kingdom of God. The history of the past and the future that is withheld from the ordinary man [is that]...

> The ancients certainly had some secret force for raising menhirs, putting in position the slabs over dolmens, hoisting enormous blocks of stone in building the temple at Baalbek, the Egyptian pyramids, and the Peruvian fortifications which they seem to have managed by somehow doing away with the weight of objects. That secret force is known as "vril" and is believed to be an element in transcendental science which makes it possible to annihilate completely the weight of anything or indeed to annihilate all active forces in the universe.

Barima states that "before the advent of Jesus, the Jews kept knowledge about the Kingdom of God secret." We know from the scriptures Jesus' parents took Him down into Egypt when the Roman ruler Herod had decreed that all Hebrew boys in Rome be killed (Matthew 2:13). It was in Egypt, according to Barima that Jesus received this special secret training from ages 12-30.

Unaware as many of us may be, the Biblical Canon is full of the transformation of Jesus to the Christ. Jesus, we have already mentioned, was human. If read carefully, it is clear that the Canon places a good deal more emphasis on His being a "Son of Man" than a "Son of God." In Acts 2:22 we are told that Jesus was a "MAN approved of God," hence the Christ being entered His body in His 30th year in Jordan and enabled Him to work "miracles, wonders, and signs" (KJV).

The name Christ corresponds with the Hebrew word Messias, and means "Anointed" or "the Messenger" and this being was thus sent from the spiritual world to convince fallen Man who he really was. The baptism of Jesus by John, signified union with the spirit and made it possible for the personality of Jesus to receive into His soul the Christ, the Logos. From the time of this incarnation, Jesus of Nazareth became the Christ.

Further statements about the earliest and most original meaning of the Kingdom of God is found in Ra Un Neter Amen's book titled *Metu Neter - The Kamitic (Egyptian) Initiation System, Vol. 2.* He states that this ancient system sought to elevate man to his divine essence.

To the African of antiquity, he says the master key to personal and social health, wealth, wisdom, and prosperity-true salvation in this life and the other - resided in the way of life in which every individual strove to awaken and develop the higher, Godlike part of being by "entering the Kingdom of God."

The fundamental principle governing [their] view of reality was the idea that Man is made in the likeness of God. Man's ability to know, to be, and to do is unlimited. To achieve such a state there were a set of teachings, observances, and practices that would assist the individual man in realizing the God within. It was made clear that man comes into the world with higher divine faculties, which are the essence of his/her salvation in an "unawakened" state. To access such power it was necessary to do more that merely profess belief in God, (Pauline thought) or seek God's help while remaining in a lowly state of ignorance and impotence, but to grow and change into our divine essence.

The point to be made here, without further indulgence, is that Jesus is unequivocally clear about what the "Kingdom of God" is in the Scriptures and His definition of the Kingdom of God coincides directly with the previously mentioned Egyptian interpretation. Jesus states in Luke 17:20-21, "The Kingdom of God does not come with your careful observation, nor will people say, 'Here it is; or There it is,' because the Kingdom of God is within you" (NIV).

So in the first instance, Jesus tells us in His own words that the Kingdom of God is not a physical thing, but a spiritual matter. You cannot see it with the eye – it is not a building, a denomination, or a place.

Secondly, these verses in Luke 17 tell us that the Kingdom is not a geographical location. You are not a part of the Kingdom of God just because you belong to a particular church in a particular place.

Jesus says that we must look within ourselves for God – not up in the sky – nor in the hills, but we must look within ourselves because that is where God resides. Where is God? Where is God's residing place? Where does God live? Jesus answers by asking the question "Did you not know that the Kingdom of God is within you?"

I Corinthians 6:19 states that your body is *the* temple of God. Your body is not just *a* temple but it is *the* temple of the living God and God's "Kingdom resides in you!!" God is **not without** you, God **is within** you!!

Now if the "kingdom" of God is in you, then the king must be in the kingdom. We have been busy outside of the kingdom, looking for the king. The Kingdom is in you, and the king is in the kingdom, where the king is supposed to be. This is what Jesus said! Read it! Read it carefully for yourself!

Out of biblical brainwashing and programming we find it almost impossible to believe that God is in us. Particularly for oppressed people who have been made to feel inferior and inadequate, this is a most absurd suggestion. For people who have been conditioned to hate themselves and to think the worst of themselves, you believe that God just can't be within you. But that makes us very hypocritical because we are always going around talking about somebody being "possessed" by the devil. We can believe that the Devil can be inside somebody, but not God. What a contradiction! Take a look at I John 4:4, a very familiar verse that many Christians quote frequently without really knowing what they are saying:

"Ye are of God, little children, and have overcome them: because greater is He that is in you, than He that is in the world" (I John 4:4).

Again take a closer look at this verse. Ye means "you are;" the preposition of means "pertaining to" or "possessed of" which means that something about you is related to God or pertains to God and that indeed you possess God. Read further!! "Greater is He that is in you means then that there is a power in you (God), that is greater than any evil force that you will face in the world.

Do you know when Jesus' enemies really decided to kill him? In the Gospel of John 10:31-35, Jesus stated that [He] and the Father [were] one. They immediately sought to stone Him to death because they felt that He "being a man" had declared Himself to be "a God." But notice Jesus responds by referencing Psalm 82. Jesus answered them, "Is it not written in your laws, I have said you are gods? If he called them gods, to whom the word of God came—and the scripture cannot be broken—what about the one whom the Father set apart as His very own and sent into the world...?" (John 10:34-36).

[God said] "They know nothing, they understand nothing. They walk around in darkness; all the foundations of the earth are shaken. I said, you are gods; you are all sons of The Most High. But you will die like mere men; you will fall like every other ruler" (NIV Psalm 82:5-7).

So we have not really known who we are; and because of that reality we don't know what we can do because we really have not been able to find God. And all of this is because we have been looking for God in the wrong places. *Therefore, we know nothing, understand nothing and walk in darkness.*

Do We Have Real Faith, Blind Faith or No Faith at All?

The theology of Paul gives us a faith we really know nothing about and do not understand. In Paul's own words, many sincere Bible believing Christians have "the form of Godliness, but deny [themselves] the power thereof" (II Tim 3:5).

Spiritual knowledge and understanding is the true basis upon which we should place our faith and belief. An "ideology" of faith without a "personal experience" of faith does not work. James, the brother of Jesus and one who had access to the Master's teachings, said that "Faith without works is dead; " that if one has knowledge and understanding it leads to action (James 2:20).

Many hungering, questing individuals have gone to their religious teachers in search of a "working knowledge" of the teachings that they have been given. They are told to just "believe" and how you just have to "have faith." Then if the deep inquiry persists, individuals are told to not question God, when they are really questioning their religious teacher. When you think about it, this is absolutely absurd. How can you be told not to question things when Jesus clearly and plainly encourages us to "seek" and [we] shall find; "knock" and the door shall be opened; and "ask" and it shall be given. You cannot put blind "faith" and "belief" in the place of "knowledge" and "understanding." The scriptures say, "my people perish for a lack of knowledge" (Hosea 4:6).

A wise person would not marry another person based on "faith" with no knowledge or understanding of what that person is like. Such wisdom is necessary because marriage is a very serious and important step in life.

Your spiritual growth, development, and welfare are even more important aspects of life. In fact, the proper development of the spiritual self undergirds the successful development of all other aspects of our lives. Jesus says in Matthew 6:33 that we are to "seek first the Kingdom of God and all His righteousness and all other things will be added unto [us]". We base our "love life" on faith and trust which comes from solid wisdom, knowledge and understanding of who our spouse is to be; but yet we follow the substitutionary teachings of Paul that require no understanding of our faith.

Jesus calls us to a life of questing after righteousness, while Paul simply says it is sufficient to rest on what Jesus has done for us.

The majority of people who profess to be Christians, I must sadly state, actually practice what I call "Paulinanity" and not Christianity. Christianity, by definition, is the religion based on the life and teachings of Jesus Christ. This definition, notwithstanding, the Apostle Paul is called the "Father of the Christian Church." Why is this so? It is because Paul is the main interpreter of the Gospels and most of the dogma and doctrine of the Christian church come not from the teachings of Jesus, but the teachings of Paul.

This becomes even more ironic when we consider that Paul never met Jesus in the flesh. Paul by his own account (Galatians 1:17) never conferred with the immediate successors of Jesus in Jerusalem (James, the brother of Jesus, Peter, John, etc.), but upon his conversion to Christianity went out into the desert of Arabia and developed his own theology. This theology became what I call the "religion about Jesus." It was a "substitutionary theory" that talks about "atonement" (in the place of) rather than "attunement" (being in touch with and in harmony with) that which Jesus talks about. There are two scriptures that make the contradiction between what Paul taught and what Jesus taught clear. Romans 10:9 captures the essence of Paul's substitutionary theory. This scripture I call the "ABCs" of orthodox Christianity (Paulinanity). It reads, "That if thou shalt confess with thy mouth the Lord Jesus and shalt believe in thine heart that God hath raised him from the dead, thou shalt be saved." It basically has come to mean to the legitimately lost, hungering souls who want to be saved from their anonymity, impersonality, and superficiality from a mean, cold, evil world to just *accept* what we tell you, just *believe* what we say, and just *confess* that you don't understand either one.

In Carl Jung's book, *The Undiscovered Self*, he refers to this phenomena of the orthodox practice of Christianity as "Mass Collectivism." So-called connoisseurs of the faith set the requirements for belonging to the church and for being "saved;" and if the aspirant does what the connoisseurs want, when they want it, and how they want it, then they are accepted as being "saved." This doctrine of Paul's is an easy, neat, systematized, closed theology, but it is not empowering, liberating, or life-changing. It absolves the individual of both accountability and self-responsibility. Jesus has "paid it all" and all one has to do is say, "I believe that He did." On the other hand, Jesus says in Matthew 16:24, "If any man will come after me let him deny himself, take up his [own] cross and follow me." Jesus then talked about a life of discipline, self-denial, self-sacrifice, work, dedication, and commitment to God through a way of living, not a way of talking.

Paul's theology has permitted very limited access to Jesus of Nazareth. Such a limitation has robbed believers of the power available to us. Is the Pauline concept of Jesus adequate? I offer an emphatic, "No!" The magnitude of the personal and social pain in our society impels us to search for a more genuine enlightenment about Jesus. Many, if not most of us, have been exposed to a quite vivid home and Sunday school series of Bible stories and "golden texts." In our childhood upbringing, these Sunday school lessons were subsequently reinforced by our parents, preachers, teachers, and the general environment we grew up in. As we groped for meaning and an identity in our teenage years, we ended up continuing to depend on the church doctrine that had ministered to our parents. Even if we joined another church, we were sure to join another "Bible-based" church that represented little, if any, difference from what we were originally taught. Many such "believers" end up passing the rest of their active lives in a "respectable, dues-paying" relationship with the church.

Ministers, for the most part, are products of the same routine. They have probably matriculated at "church-related or indoctrinated" seminaries. Such seminaries or Bible colleges are given subtle, and not so subtle, directions through financial gifts of support about what should be taught. Other ministers are just "jack-leg" preachers, basically untrained, unlettered individuals who simply mimic the theology of orthodoxy.

Clearly, there is little or no tolerance for radicalism. If a preacher wants to pastor a church, he has to, so to speak, "tow the line." This cycle continues to be repeated from generation to generation today because of the environmentally and culturally supported belief in the primacy of the Bible. America has always pointed to her "Judeo-Christian" tradition and the chief source of this tradition has been historically acknowledged to be the Bible. Therefore, there has been little analysis of the Bible for fear of hell and damnation (loss of personal salvation). One would rarely opt to question, evaluate, or investigate church tutelage. We have been programmed to believe that the church alone has the right answers to guarantee our salvation and eternal life. So, while we have had many questions about faith, we have been afraid to ask. While we have had many baffling enigmas in our "Christian walk," we have been afraid to ask for answers. As we read the books of the Bible there are unnumbered situations and statements we have not understood. There are experiences so removed, so uncomfortable to realities in our own everyday experiences that they have left us in a state of bewilderment. The only explanation anyone has ever given us for their incredibility is "It's a mystery." "It is not for us to understand everything in the Bible." "Don't question, just believe" and/or "some things we won't understand until the 'sweet bye and bye'."

This "Bible-mystery syndrome" has become socialized, institutionalized, and gloried as "faith." We need only look around us to see that such a blind believing, Biblically-derived mystery is being challenged like never before. In the African American community, in particular, and the larger society, in general, our young people (and many adults) are looking for deeper meaning. Prior to the 1950s in the African American community, the exception was the youth who did not attend church. Jawanza Kunjufu reports in his book, *Adam Where Are You?* that in the 1950s, eight out of ten African American youth were involved in some church, temple, mosque, or synagogue. But now, that number has dwindled to about three out of ten. To such persons, the biblical explanation that they have been given just does not cover the facts or meet their needs.

A Look at the Canon

To be free to discover some deeper Spiritual Dynamics in the Bible which have powerful personal implications, we must rise above strict theological limits. To do so, we must raise the question of the Canon.

The "closing of the Canon" (see earlier statements on the Council of Nicea in AD 325), is at odds with a large range of human realities. In the first place, to close the Canon is to say God is dead. If God is dead, then God is not God. If God is no longer speaking or revealing Himself in contemporary times, and if we are limited to what He said several thousand years ago, then God *is* dead. Closing the Canon also suggests that "Christian" experience is valid only within the confines of the Canon. It suggests to us and assumes for us that the "revealed" character of the Christian experience allows no room for improvement or change. The Canon has been revered by the Church as "immutable and perfect." Therefore, "communicating the Gospel" becomes the freedom to only intellectualize the details sanctified within the limits of the Canon.

Why is the Canon so Entrenched?

The main reason is because primary authority has been vested in prophets, apostles, and teachers. No one else was given the authority or right to speak about scripture. The people were taught by them to worship the Bible, rather than study the Bible in order to extract Spiritual Dynamics. Such a perspective was largely perpetuated for political control and social domination. Today we must use the Bible not to worship, as we would God, but as an inimitable point of departure for crucial insights into the ways and means of our spiritual development and vision. We must always remember that the Bible is not God, but the Word of God. We profit from the truth of the Bible and we cannot then approach it with pious literalism or rejecting cynicism. If we do either, we will rob ourselves of the Bible's depths and rich treasure. Christian theology has promulgated a rigidity which has insisted that we understand reality only in the reported disclosures of the personalities in the Canon.

As my mentor, the late Dr. Leon Wright, stated in his book, *From Cult to Cosmos - Can Jesus be Saved?* "the real task is to identify the *dynamics* of interplay between God and those in fellowship with Him." We must understand the Spiritual Dynamics that the personalities of the scriptures employed to attain the level of spiritual ascendancy they manifested. As well, we have the responsibility of learning the tentative struggle that moved them from narrow perspectives to deeper proportions of faith. It is quite unfortunate that we have been conditioned to use the Bible as some magical amulet or talisman. Such object worship shrouds in ambiguity the cosmic principles in the scriptures. There is no single book or series of books, however ancient or recent, that can finally and exhaustively disclose God's infinite mind. It is time that we make room alongside those 66 books that are so fiercely defended and finalized as the "Bible" for current experiences and discoveries about God and man. This will allow the living Word of God to be continuously experienced and recorded as the Word of God. If God is alive, it then means that He is still speaking and still revealing Himself in contemporary times.

Dr. Wright again states that, "the message of the Bible that is open for wider dissemination is that the universe is alive, the bush is always burning, the Heavens are always open."

The accounts in the Bible all suggest the availability of similar resources for every man. We need only earnestly ask, probe, hunger and thirst after the righteousness. We must see the Bible as a point of departure toward a supremely vital concept and experience of God. Ideally, the Bible confronts us today with the optimum challenge to avail ourselves of the opportunity and the right to locate and tap into this resource. Our attempt in discussing the teachings of Paul is not to impeach his unique credentials. However, we must revisit Paul because it is Paul's extensions and elaboration on the teachings of Jesus that constitute the essential basis of Christian dogma today. It is largely due to the Pauline thought that the Jesus of history, the prophet of Nazareth has become the "Christ of Faith." It is Paul who gave us intensive dogmatic rigidities on the matters of slavery, women, and marriage. Paul has been identified with bigotry, anti-feminism, escapist asceticism, and an uniformed, irrelevant sexual perspective. We know all of this and yet we are reluctant to openly test the implications of Paul's teachings for today's world. In the chaotic confusion of today's world, many people come to the church for resources to help them achieve a healthy resilience from their pain. The conventional orthodoxy of Pauline thought just does not satisfy. Certain finalities of Paul must be responded to dynamically or more and more will be lost to an inadequate Christian faith. The zeal to "defend" the faith has superseded the desire to "deliver" the fallen. Passionate supporters of the Pauline dictum, "Jesus is Lord," have claimed a "once and for all" errant mentality about Paul's teachings which has resulted in ultimatizing and making Paul's concepts and ideas sacrosanct.

Paulinanity, though pompously and academically structured, has no real power. As we examine Pauline thought over and against the teachings of Jesus, I suspect that we will find a truer, more relevantly powerful disclosure of our reality as beings created in the image of God. What

I am suggesting runs afoul of the generally accepted beliefs. Paul gives us a theological perpetuation of Jesus of Nazareth wholly alien to Jesus' own appropriation of Himself. After the death of Jesus, a kind of Christological definition of Jesus came into vogue. This definition is called the "Kerygma." Kerygma deals only with the birth, death, burial and resurrection of Jesus. It speaks little, if at all, about the historical figure named Jesus. A crucial question for the downtrodden, for whom Jesus came, is: Just how critical is this Jesus of History who has been largely "overlooked, omitted, and interred?" In the introduction of Dr. Howard Thurman's classic book, *Jesus and The Disinherited*, he states "the significance of the religion of Jesus to people with their backs against the wall [is] . . . crucial." He further states that it is an emphasis that has always been lacking. It is this failure that makes Christianity so impotent to "radically" and "effectively" deal with the issue of race and national origin. Dr. Thurman raised the question of whether the "impotency [is] due to a betrayal of the genius of the religion, or is it due to a basic weakness in the religion itself." He suggests, and I concur, that "the many and varied interpretations dealing with the teachings and the life of Jesus of Nazareth . . [have] been 'sterile' and of little avail." The conventional word about Jesus, according to Dr. Thurman, has been "muffled, confused and vague."

It was in 1949, when the aforementioned book was published that Thurman observed that few sermons dealt with what the message of Jesus says to the poor masses (the majority of people in the world). The critical question to be asked is: What does the Christian faith (religion of Jesus) say to the disinherited, the poor and the dispossessed? What does it offer to meet their needs? These questions are still just as relevant today as they were some fifty years ago. The answer to these questions remains the "most important religious question of modern life." Within this context historical Christian dogma and doctrine must be revisited, especially the teachings of Paul. Paul's admonition in Ephesians 6:5 "Slaves be obedient to your master" was one of the main scriptures used by slave masters in their "customized" version of Christianity to make slaves more "docile and obedient." In I Corinthians 7:9 Paul speaks on the issue of sex and marriage. He states "it is better to marry than to burn." Whether using the term burn means to "burn in hell" or to "burn with lust," both are wrong reasons to get married. It is this silly notion (getting married to satisfy the sexual urge) that has caused many to marry without love and commitment and end up with a harsh divorce. We know all of this and yet we are still reluctant to openly test the implications of Paul's thinking for today's world.

If you are a bibliolatrist (worshipper of the Bible) this will frighten you. If you desire to be a true follower of Jesus, it will ultimately challenge and enlighten you. We must understand the spirituality of Paul, but reject the dogma. We must recover the cosmic-awareness of the African Hebrew Jesus. We must, armed with such a cosmic awareness, search out a contemporary understanding of life that Paul's kerygmatic message has served to limit. We must not use as infallible revelation what Paul legitimately taught in a genuine effort to make Jesus real, supreme and ultimate for the time in which He lived. We must be consistently aware that Paul was competing against strong philosophies and belief systems that promoted a supposed supremacy to all other religious thought.

Our choice is between an allegiance to a "pre-existent, co-eternal Lord," (II Cor. 5:16-20), who died for all or to reconsider the man called Jesus who has been so effectively obscured by the more awesome claims of Lordship. The theology of Paul is neat and systematized but not empowering or life-changing. A study of the life of Jesus will lead to a bold, enlightened existence. The question to be raised again is: If Christianity is the religion based on the life and teachings of Jesus, why is Paul called the "Father of the Christian Church"? The answer, as we have previously mentioned, is because the theology of the Christian church is based on the teachings of Paul. Jesus urged a loyalty to God which was to be the prime characteristic of His followers. Such an understanding of one's relationship to God needs no "free gift" on a cross. Rather, it requires bearing our own cross, the commitment to total submission and surrender to the will of God.

My former professor of the New Testament at Howard University School of Divinity stated in his book, *From Cult to Cosmos: Can Jesus be Saved?* that, "Jesus enjoins man to aspire to the achievement of spiritual perfection." The practice of orthodox Christianity does not do this. Earlier in this writing, we stated that Paul never met Jesus. Paul went out into the deserts of Arabia (see Galatians 1:17) and developed his own theology. Why did Paul not consult with the immediate followers of Jesus, the followers of Jesus such as Peter, John, et al? How did Paul manage to gain a greater hearing than these immediate followers? The fact is, Paul was a very learned man. He studied Pharisaic law under the great legal mind of Gamaliel. By contrast, the immediate followers of Jesus were unlearned, grassroots laborers. Therefore, by the sheer eloquence of his tongue, the fact that he carried his message of Jesus to uninformed Gentiles, allowed Paul to amass a great following. We must, as well, consider the "psychological furniture" of the time that caused Paul to develop his conceptualization of Jesus. Remember when Jesus was crucified, His followers expected Him to return in just a few days. They had little concern for the affairs on earth because they expected the imminent return of Jesus. There was no need to hoard material things or have any type of organizational structure because Jesus would soon return and they would go with Him to Heaven. Well, the days turned to weeks, weeks into months, and months into years. It then became necessary, as it does whenever a body of people come together for any extended length of time, for an organizational structure, for rules, regulations and requirements for membership to be institutionalized. Paul, therefore, established some requirements (for being "saved") for membership. Jesus never asked anyone: "Are you saved?" He was always ministering to people, pointing them to a relationship with God. Jesus, literally and simultaneously, saw man as Son of Man and the Son of God, in the same degree. This sensitivity was available to any individual who "hungered" and "thirst" in the God-ward quest. Not so with Paul! Paul taught and espoused a theology which contended that such a depth of awareness was peculiar and exclusive to Jesus. Jesus, being crucified, His disciples, not only unlearned but afraid, made way for Paul to ascend as the chief spokesperson for the Christian Church. However, this was not accomplished without Paul being challenged and confronted by Jesus' disciples for teaching contrary to what Jesus had taught them. In Acts 21:20-26, the Apostle Paul is charged by the elders at Jerusalem (James, the brother of Jesus, Peter, et al.) to shave his head and admit to the gathering crowd of angry Jews that he was sorry for teaching the Gentiles that they did not have to be circumcised. Paul, you see, wanted to identify with his Gentile oppressors. Though he was a Black Jew, Rev. Albert Cleage says in his book, *Black Christian Nationalism-New Directions for the Black Church:*

> ...he wanted to identify with his White Gentile oppressors. The Disciples who remained in Jerusalem knew that he was preaching a false doctrine that had nothing at all to do with the Jesus with whom they had walked and talked. They tried to hold him accountable for his White corruptions. He tricked them just as people do today. He raised money from the churches he had organized and went back to Jerusalem with enough money to

persuade the original Disciples to overlook the fact that what he was teaching was a false doctrine. Paul does not follow in the footsteps of Jesus.

Paul had been forewarned that he would be attacked and jailed upon entering Jerusalem. At that he vehemently stated that not only was he going, but if necessary he was ready to die for his beliefs. However, the scriptures are clear that upon his arrival to Jerusalem he did consent to do what the elders told him to do because he was afraid. As well, being men of honesty and integrity, the Jerusalem elders would not command Paul to say something that they did not really believe to be correct. Thus, we are left with the conclusion that these immediate followers of Jesus felt that it was both essential and necessary for Paul to correct the error of teaching against circumcision. The scripture states that Paul did as he was told. He was ultimately jailed and threatened with death. Because of Paul's eloquence of tongue, he was able to escape. It is quite interesting to wonder what the dominant theology of the Christian church would be if the immediate followers of Jesus had gained ascendancy (power) over Paul as the early leaders of the church. Being unlearned they just could not compete with Paul. Therefore after this encounter, Paul continued to travel extensively preaching and teaching his own theology.

What was the Religion of Jesus?

The religion of Jesus leads one to a continually embattled quest for meaning and purpose. This then leads to an emboldening, enlightening, empowering existence. Paul's interpretation of the religion of Jesus does not develop the individual personality, improve society, or make the world a better place. The quest for the historical Jesus (religion of Jesus) leads us to cosmic, groundbreaking experiences regarding the nature and destiny of man. We have relied, too heavily, on the notion that "Jesus is Lord" at the cost of being unaware of the pregnant possibilities within our nature as beings in the image of God.

Every man is a "son of man" and a "son of God." Paul's ideas of Jesus as the special and exclusive Son of God is not in conformity with the sayings and the teachings of Jesus. In the Bible the expression, "Son of God," was used for many earlier prophets. For instance, Israel was called the "Son of God" in the Book of Exodus 4:22. "And thou shalt say unto Pharaoh, Thus, said the Lord, Israel is my son, My First born." (Psalm 2:7) says "I will declare the decree the Lord hath said unto me, thou art my Son, this day have I begotten thee." A little later in the Bible,

Solomon was also called the Son of God. I Chronicles 22:10 states, "He shall build an house for my Name; and he shall be my son, and I will be his Father and I will establish the throne of his Kingdom over Israel forever." This phrase only means nearness to God in love. Jesus, on whom Christianity *should* be based, said that every man who did the will of the Father in Heaven was a Son of God. It was devout living, and kind and merciful behavior that made a man worthy of being called the Son of God. Is this not what Jesus states in Matthew 5:44-45? "Love your enemies. . . that ye may be the children of your Father which is in Heaven." And, in Matthew 5:9: "Blessed are the peacemakers, for they shall be called the Sons of God." These sayings are clear as to what Jesus meant. In view of this, there is no justification for regarding Jesus as the Son of God in an exclusive or unique sense. Jesus mostly called Himself a "Son of Man." When he did refer to Himself as a "Son of God," it was no doubt that it was in the same sense that Adam, Israel, David, and Solomon each had been called the "Son of God." Rev. Dr. Potter states in his book on the Nag-Hammadi discoveries that:

> one thing is emerging from the study of the (Dead Sea) Scrolls—namely, that the beliefs, teachings, and practices of Jesus Himself, although not identical in all respects of those of the Essene school that he probably attended during the "silent years," were apparently closer to those of the Essene than to those of the bishops of the ecumenical council which determined the Nicene Creed of orthodox Christianity. Jesus called himself the Son of Man; they called him the Son of God, the second person of the Trinity, Very God of Very God. It is most doubtful if the Essenes or Jesus himself would have agreed with that.

In John 10:34-36 the remarks of Jesus will further show that it was only in a metaphorical sense that Jesus called Himself a "Son of God."

> Jesus answered them, "Is it not written in your law, I said, Ye are gods? If he called them gods, unto whom the word of God came, and the scripture cannot be broken; say ye of him whom the Father hath sanctified and sent into the world, Thou blasphemest because I said I am the Son of God?"

In order to come into our "Sonship," we must, as Jesus, have a very intense mystical personal encounter with the Father to understand the actualities that Jesus talked about. We must go back to Jesus!! After we go back to Jesus, we must do like Jesus did, then we will have the same power Jesus has. In John 14:12 Jesus says, "Marvel not at the things I do because greater things than these shall ye do." We need information about ourselves and the wider reality of which we are a part. All of us are born with the "dunamis" (Greek for raw power). All we need to realize is that we have the "exorcia" (the authority) to use that power. As long as we allow Christian scholars to insist upon locking all faith within biblical confines, we will learn little of the personal and mystical power Jesus taught and manifested.

Pauline dogma and doctrine have been allowed to supply both the content and the potential of the Christian experience. The vital question about who Jesus is must always remain open!! Within the orthodoxy of Christianity (Pauline thought) there is no goal except to sit around and be saved. There is total absolving of all accountability and responsibility. The principal emphasis of Jesus' teaching, on the other hand, was an ethical works related thrust which has been muted in favor of sacramental concessions to "human frailty." Jesus pointed the way for a universal applicable spiritual direction for man. He moved from being "Jesus of Nazareth" to "Jesus, God Man (the Christ)." The divine credentials of Jesus have been embellished to the exclusion of the exceptional "Jesus, the Man." Several scriptures are usually referenced to promote Jesus, exclusively, as the Son of God. Thus it stated in 1 Timothy 2:5, "For there is one God, and one mediator between God and men, the man Jesus Christ." In Acts 4:12, "Neither is there salvation in any other: For there is none other name under Heaven given among men, whereby we must be saved." A very important reference is John 14:6, which states "Jesus saith unto him, I am the way, the truth, and the life, no man cometh unto the Father, but by me."

I submit that all of this "one and only" talk pertains more to the medium used than the core message. There was no other way, no other language for these early saints to talk about what Jesus had done for them. Thus, what Jesus meant to them was "love language." It is like a person saying "My mother is the sweetest mother in the world." This is just a feeble attempt to define the undefinable. How does one really explain how much their mother means to them? How does somebody explain the life-changing, life-saving experience of him who has been snatched from the depths of hell? To that person who has been saved that savior is "the one and only" savior.

Secondly, "the one-and-only" talk is survival language. These Christians had minority status in the Roman Empire. In defining Jesus in absolute terms, they cut out for themselves a distinct difference from other religions. Such language also evoked a total commitment that would hold them in the face of ridicule, competition, or persecution.

Who, then, is Jesus?

Jesus represents the fulfillment of what we can be as human beings. We are more importantly transcendent Spiritual Beings. In Jesus, human nature is at the point that man is always trying to reach. The incarnation of God in the man Jesus of Nazareth is the realization of the highest possibility of man's being. Jesus is the symbol that provides the assurance that the infinite hopes and striving of our human nature are not in vain. It is possible for all humans to be one with the Father God, even as Jesus is. (Reference John 17:21). Jesus prayed "that they all may be one as thou Father, art in me, and I in thee, that they also may be one in us."

What does this say about Personal Commitment?

Many Christians feel that their faith is threatened by the fact that Jesus may or may not be the definitive, normative revelation; that there may be other saviors and other incarnations. Deep down, many of us feel that for something to be true it has to be the *only* truth. This is particularly true of the Eurocentric mindset. The Eurocentric presupposition is that its culture is so superior that when exposed to any other culture, it is always the best, most superior, the truest. This is why it is very important for African Americans to understand the henotheistic belief of traditional African religion which does not deny or reject the existence of other belief systems so long as they do not interfere with one's own beliefs.

What brings a person to have faith in, and a commitment to Jesus is a transforming experience, not the idea that Jesus alone is revelation and grace. You can be totally committed to your own religion, even though you know that there are other religions that have value. Absolute exclusivity is neither healthy nor honest. We need to be secure in our own identity and more committed to its unifying vision. The more we do this the more we will be able to tolerate and accept other visions and the closer we will be to God. Religious intolerance is a sign of spiritual immaturity.

We are always persuaded by those who speak with deep conviction of what their savior has done for them. We are not persuaded by those who tell us that "my savior is bigger than your savior." Jesus had the right relationship with the Father, one of obedience and submission to the

Father. He was attuned. This relationship is available to any individual who "hungers" and "thirsts." It is divine law that Jesus teaches us that the cosmos, the universe, is constructed such that it guarantees fulfill-ment of any and every effort to divine son-ship/daughter-ship. We are all sons (prodigal sons) who have turned our backs on God. We can "come to ourselves!!" Blessed are they which do hunger and thirst after righteousness! For they shall be filled" (Matthew 5:6).

What Jesus Taught
The Beatitudes

Chapter V

Jesus is, or should be the number one authority for how we live the Christian life. As we mentioned in chapter one, Christianity is by definition the religion based on the life and teachings of Jesus Christ. Jesus is the central figure of the Christian faith – not Paul, not the Old Testament prophets – Jesus!!

The life of Jesus, and the teachings attributed to Him have had tremendous influence over people during the course of history.

As such no more important questions can be raised than the following. What <u>was</u> most important to Jesus? What <u>did</u> Jesus teach? What <u>did</u> Jesus say? What <u>was</u> vital and crucial to Jesus as the foundation of his teachings? Has Christianity, as it has been practiced for about twenty centuries, really expressed and adequately represented His ideas? Does Christianity today present His message to the world? And, if Jesus came back today – what would he say about the plethora of "Christian" denominations and their varied dogma and doctrine?

The message which Jesus taught and demonstrated was simple, direct concise, and yet a perfect statement of the nature of God, man, and of life, and of the relationship that exists between all three.

Not only that, but what Jesus taught was not mere academic, intellectual masturbation, but practical methods for spiritual development and successful living. Jesus not only tells us why we fail, why we succumb to negativity, why we become destitute and impoverished; but more important than any of these things, He tells us how all the evils of the world can be overcome, and how we can bring true happiness, prosperity and blessings into our lives and into the lives of others.

The first thing we must acknowledge is a fact of fundamental importance, because it means breaking away from Christian orthodoxy (the Paulinanity we have previously discussed) and getting in touch with the lessons that Jesus taught.

The plain fact is that Jesus taught no theology whatever. His teaching is entirely spiritual or metaphysical. It may surprise you, but all of the doctrines and theologies of the churches are human inventions, built up by their inventors out of their own mentalities. There is absolutely no system of theology or doctrine to be found in the Bible; it simply is not there. For many different reasons, religious people manufactured the theology that promoted their social, economic, and political aspirations. In the introduction to Dr. Ani's book, *Yurugu*, noted African American historian Dr. John Henry Clarke, notes that:

> ... the world has been controlled by a form of European Nationalism.... They have declared most things primitive that they could not understand. They have laughed at the Gods of other people. This cruelty was compounded when, through propaganda and the misuse of the Bible, they taught other people to laugh at their chosen Gods and adopt the God of their conqueror.... The emergence of Europeans or White people as the handlers of world power and their ability to convince millions of people that this is the way things should be is the greatest single propaganda miracle in history.... The European conquest of the mind of most of the people of Africa and Asia is their greatest achievement.

The European race now, throughout the two millenniums during which the race has dominated and molded the destinies of the entire world, culturally, socially, and politically have interpreted, reinterpreted and "customized" the religion of Jesus to satisfy their own vested interests. And most of us call ourselves "Christians" because we were taught by our parents to be "Christians." Our parents called themselves "Christians" because their parents called themselves "Christians."

But where did they get their teachings about Christianity? Who gave our foreparents their teachings about Christianity? We were taught what we know about Christianity by our slavemaster. We have already mentioned how in 1842 Rev. C. Colquit Jones developed a "customized version" of Christianity for Negro slaves that would, in his words, not liberate us but would make Blacks "more docile," "more subservient" and "more obedient" than any whip or chains.

And our foreparents accepted these teachings with no questions asked. When Rev. Richard Allen and Rev. Absalom Jones started the first Black churches in America, there was no question or contention over the foundational doctrine and dogma of the White slavemaster's interpretation of Christianity, but only over whether they would use the White Methodist or the White Episcopalian methodology. So, as oppressed people in America, we did not ever receive the true teachings of Jesus. History bears out the fact that ever since we were brought to this country as slaves, White Christians sought to kill our minds, our bodies and our spirits in every manner conceivable.

So why would those who, throughout our history in America, have spent the majority of their time trying to kill us and our minds, at the same time give us a Gospel of Jesus that would bring us and our minds back to life? That would make absolutely no sense. How could the same people, or (why) would the same people, who have deliberately tried to annihilate us, turn around and show us the *true* path to God that Jesus really taught?

There is great truth and revelation in the message that was taught by Jesus. But what I am saying is that Christianity, as we know it, is only the White slavemaster's teachings of what and who God is, and who we are. We have never been really taught the true teachings of Jesus. We have been given the teachings of our oppressor, with Jesus' name on it. Richard Tawney in his book, *Religion and the Rise of Capitalism,* documents very well how distorted Christianity served the European in his domination of the world. Max Weber offers as well a picture of a very clear relationship between the founding of Protestantism and the development/advancement of Western capitalism. In the book, *The Protestant Ethic and the Spirit of Capitalism,* Weber shows that there is a relationship between the nature and the theology of the Catholic Church and certain economic structures. Amos Wilson in his book, *The Falsification of African Consciousness,* says:

> So whether you want to recognize it or not, the Church and Religion are intimately related to the economic and social structure... This means that we, as Black people, have the right to redefine the Church in ways that advance our interests, not only economic interests but social, political, and many other interests in our lives. We need to look at the Church in the context of Afrikan life and see how the church (without losing its spiritual and ethical mission) can also function to enhance Afrikan economic, social, and political life.... If we study the theology and the life of Jesus, we will read of His struggle with the ideology coming out of the major religious establishment of His time. That establishment was also a part of an economic order and structure that rationalized and idealized the then economic structure in such a way that people were literally forced into poverty, and in many instances forced into sin and degradation.
>
> The Church, by restructuring itself and by revising its view of itself economically, and its role economically, not only enhances

the material well-being of the people, but can also better carries out its spiritual/ethical function as an institution.

We must stop fighting each other over European ideologies and base our religious ideology upon a profound analysis of the true teachings of Jesus and upon our own history and experience. Oppressed people cannot continue to hold onto "imported, foreign theology" that was "given" to us by our oppressor.

We *must* acquire an African-centered theology, developed first out of the message and life of the Jesus of History with the infusion of a theology developed out of our own history and experience. We need an Africentric church with an Africentric theology.

Even today, African American churches still teach this slave-taught version of Christianity. A church is not Africentric because it has Kente cloth-draped chairs, a red, black and green hymnal or even Black images on the walls of the church, if it still teaches the same Christian dogma perpetuated by the slavemaster.

The teachings of orthodox Christianity conflict with what Jesus taught. The teachings of Christianity are not the religion that Jesus practiced in the Bible. The Bible is the history and the prophecy of Black people. We must therefore read it from a Black theological perspective, not from a White, oppressive theological perspective.

Jesus insisted upon a certain spirit in one's conduct, and He was careful to teach principles only, knowing that when the spirit is right, details will take care of themselves; and that, in fact, "the letter killeth, but the spirit giveth life" (II Corinthians 3:6).

Yet, in spite of this, the history of orthodox Christianity is largely made up of attempts to enforce all sorts of external observances upon people. Jesus has been sadly misinterpreted and misunderstood. Equally unfortunate is the fact that human nature would rather blindly believe something rather than labor in searching the scriptures for truth.

Many well-intentioned, sincere men and women have crowned themselves as authoritative Christian leaders, with the most imposing and pretentious titles, elaborate and gorgeous vestments, and crafted credentials to give themselves credence and authority to "Lord" over the people.

Many Christians operating out of "blind faith" and lacking the "Spiritual understanding" of the Scriptures reject the miraculous acts of Jesus or at least do not believe them. Such persons attribute the miracles of Jesus to the usual fantastic legends that center on all great historical fig-

The Order of Service

The Organ Prelude-------------------------- Mrs. Valerie Mills-Cooper.

The Processional --Clergy & Family

The Opening Hymn ---

Blessed Assurance (*)

The Prayer of Consolation------------------------------- Min. Kevin Graves.

The Scripture Reading:

The OT -- Mr. George Graves Sr.

Job 19:25-27

The NT --Ms. Katherine Gross

St. John 14:1-6

The Selection--Ms. Katherine Gross

The Words of Comfort-----------------------------------Visiting Clergy,
Family and Friends

The Obituary--Mr. George Trotter

The Solo--Mrs. Viola Johnson

The Eulogy --------------------------------------Rev. Reginald Tarpley, Pastor

The Recessional/ Hymn ------------------------------------Hymn

When We All Get To Heaven (*)

The Hymnal to be announced (*)

In loving Memory

of

Catina Dominique Gilmore

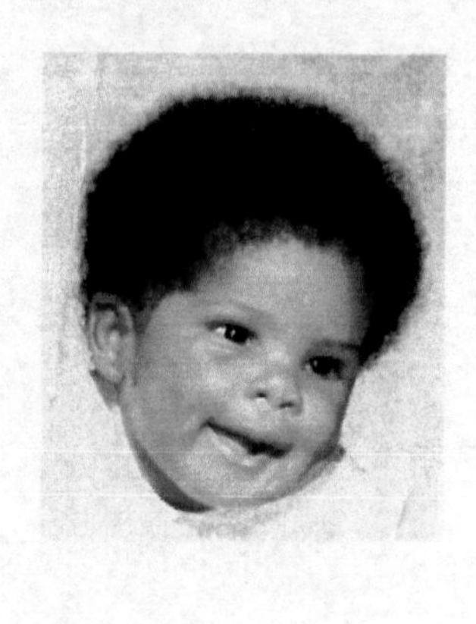

Sunrise
July 7, 1972

Sunset
October 1, 2011

Home going Services
October 10, 2011

Wake: 10:30 AM **Funeral: 11:00 AM**

In the sanctuary of
Cecil Memorial United Methodist Church
15 Parole Street
Annapolis, Maryland 21401

Officiating Minister:
The Reverend Reginald Tarpley, Pastor

Words from the Pastor

"…and it doth not yet appear what we shall be: but we know that, when he shall appear, we shall be like him; for we shall see him as he is (1 John. 3:2)."

Be of good cheer and trust in the comforts of the Lord. May the peace of our Lord and Saviour, Jesus Christ, dwell with you richly. Amen.

Pallbearers

--Relatives & Close friends--

Acknowledgements

The family expresses their sincere appreciation for all acts of kindness extended to them during their hour of sorrow.

Interment

Bestgate Memorial Park
1814 Bestgate Road
Annapolis, Maryland 21401

Repast

The family will receive relatives and friends at the repast, immediately following the interment, in the Cecil Memorial UMC's Fellowship hall.

Entrusted Professional Services and Comfort

William Reese & Sons Mortuary, P.A.
1922 Forest Drive
Annapolis, Maryland 21401

✝

The Obituary

Catina Dominique Gilmore, affectionately known as Tina, departed this life on October 1, 2011. Tina was born to Janny (Frances) Gilmore and the late Eddie L. Gilmore on July 7, 1972 in Baltimore Md.

Catina graduated in 1991 from Annapolis High School. Catina enjoyed the art of cosmetology and loved doing the ladies hair. She really appreciated all of the compliments they would bestow upon her for their beautiful hairdos. Tina liked to brag about her culinary skills especially her delicious meatloaf and kale. Tina also prided herself on her exceptional people skills. Tina knew everybody and everybody knew Tina.

Catina leaves fond memories by her loving mother Janny "Frances" Gilmore her daughter, Nashell Smith, three sons, Cornell Contee, Eerric Hinton and Vick Chance, grandson D'Ari Parker, one brother, Eddie L. Gilmore Jr and one sister, Ashley J. Gilmore, grandmothers, Lorraine Graves of Annapolis, Md and Florence Gilmore-Kersee of Los Angeles, Calif, nine aunts, seven uncles, one great aunt, one great, great aunt, one great uncle, one great, great uncle and a host of nieces, nephews cousins and friends.

✞

Put your trust in the Lord and lean not to your own understanding. In all your ways acknowledge the lord, and He will direct your path (Proverbs 3: 5-6).

Medical Records
FAX 410-315-9150

Goodbye Mother

My mother was a good Mommy, She was there when I needed her the most. My mom had a good spirit. she was there when I didn't have a Father or Dad to watch my little brother and I. I've known my Mother for 11years. I can remember all the fun times we had together , they were great .But now I know I may not be able to touch her or see her, but this I do KNOW, YOU WILL ALWAYS BE IN OUR HEARTS!!!!!!!!.

Your loving Son,

Eerric

ures or simply relegate such experience to "things that happened back then, but do not happen today."

But if the miracles did not happen, the Gospel loses its real significance. Jesus taught and did many things that are in flat contradiction to rational thinking.

The miracles did happen and He further said, referring to those who would really study and practice His teaching: "The works that I do, ye shall do, and greater works" (John 14:12).

The Sermon on the Mount, in Matthew 5, 6, and 7, are the most important teachings of Jesus as to how to be His follower. These lessons of Jesus must, however, have a spiritual interpretation. It is "spiritual" not 'intellectual" understanding, that unlocks the mystery of the teachings of Jesus. Jesus performed miracles to prove to us that we, too, can overcome limitations.

With a spiritual understanding of the Bible, we can discard the tendency to worship the Bible in uninformed literalism, and yet understand that the Bible is really the most precious and most authentic possession we can have. The teachings of Jesus are rich in Spiritual Dynamics – practical spiritual laws that will enable us to develop spiritual power.

Externally, the Bible is a collection of inspired documents written by all kinds of men, in all kinds of situations, over hundreds of years. The documents as we have them are seldom originals, but translations, redactions and compilations of older fragments.

This in no wise, however, affects the spiritual purpose of the Bible in the slightest. It is in fact, irrelevant. The Bible, even as we have it, is an inexhaustible reservoir of spiritual truth, compiled under divine inspiration, and the actual route by which it reached its present form does not matter. This is why John 16:13 states, "Howbeit, when the spirit is come, it will lead you and guide you into all truth." The purpose of studying the Bible is to be led into a personal spiritual encounter. What modern day theologians call "Higher Criticism" concerns itself with externals completely overlooking the Spiritual content of the scriptures, and from the Spiritual point of view is of no value.

History, biography, and poetic forms are various mediums through which the spiritual message is given in the Bible. Parables, especially, are used by Jesus to convey spiritual truth. The Bible gives us spiritual truth!! And that truth is the fact that man's thought can and does have influence on his entire outer world. Man's physical body, the circumstances and situations of life, and even his physical environment are amenable to his thought. The thoughts that occupy our minds are molding our destiny everyday. The fact is that our entire life's experience is but the outer expression of inner thought.

We can therefore choose the kind of thoughts that we entertain. In fact, we *do* choose. Our lives are, therefore, the result of the kind of thoughts we have chosen to hold.

We do not, as many of us have been taught, suffer for somebody else's (Adam) original sin, but the reaping of the harvest that we ourselves have sown (Proverbs 23:7).

We have free will which lies in our choice of thought.

This is the essence of what Jesus taught. Jesus not only taught this truth, but also demonstrated it in His life. Jesus proves everything He taught, even through the overcoming of death. It is as well the underlying message of the entire Gospel.

Jesus, by surmounting every type of limitation to which man is subject, including death, performed a work of uniqueness and inestimable value, and is therefore justly called the Savior of the World.

In the Sermon on the Mount, He sums up the whole of His teachings in a series of lectures. Thus in Matthew 5, 6, and 7 is almost a perfect cataloging of the religion of Jesus Christ. Once the true meaning of these teachings is grasped, it is only necessary to begin putting it faithfully into practice to get results. The measure and extent of the results will be in direct proportion to the sincerity and the thoroughness with which they are practiced.

If you really wish to change your life, to become a different person altogether – if you really do want health and peace of mind, and spiritual development, then let Jesus, in the Sermon on the Mount, show you how to get it done.

What are The Beatitudes?

The Beatitudes are eight verses that are a general summary of the whole Christian teaching. They summarize the spirit of the teaching of Jesus rather than the letter.

> And seeing the multitudes, he went up into a mountain, and when he was set, his disciples came unto him:
> And he opened his mouth, and taught them, saying,
> Blessed are the poor in spirit: for theirs is the kingdom of heaven.
> Blessed are they that mourn: for they shall be comforted.
> Blessed are the meek: for they shall inherit the earth. Blessed

> are they which do hunger and thirst after righteousness: for they shall be filled. Blessed are the merciful: for they shall obtain mercy. Blessed are the pure in heart: for they shall see God. Blessed are the peacemakers: for they shall be called the children of God. Blessed are they which are persecuted for righteousness sake: for theirs is the kingdom of heaven.
> Blessed are ye, when men shall revile you and persecute you, and shall say all manner of evil against you falsely, for my sake (Matthew 5:1-11).

Jesus concerned Himself exclusively with the teaching of general principles and these general principles always had to do with the mental states, for He knew that if one's mental state is right, everything else must be right too; whereas, if it is wrong, nothing else can be right.

The policy of Jesus contrasts with the Pharisees' appalling code of outward detailed observances. He worked to wean people from relying upon outer things, either for pleasurable gratification or for spiritual salvation and to inculcate a new attitude of mind that is set forth in The Beatitudes.

The Beatitudes thus deal with the right attitude, the right mental state, or the right motive for behavior. They speak to the proper development of the inner self.

Beatitude 1: "Blessed *are* the poor in spirit: for theirs is the kingdom of heaven."

We must start with the reality that the Bible is written in a peculiar idiom of its own, and that terms, expressions, and actual words are used in a way distinctly different from our everyday usage. As well, certain English words have changed in meaning since the Bible was translated.

Any living language is constantly changing. Many words used in the King James Version, for example, are today almost unknown. Examples are "neesings," "besom," and "wist". Other words have changed their meaning totally. For example, <u>let</u> formerly meant "to hinder" (Romans 1:13), but now it means "to permit." Another word that has changed meaning is <u>conversation</u>. Today it means "talk," but to the English people of King James' day it meant "the whole way of living." Unless we recognize that old meaning, we miss the point of such passages as II Peter 2:7 and 3:11.

Because the Bible is a textbook on *Spirituality, a manual for growth of the Spirit*, it looks at all questions from this perspective. It takes the broadest view of every subject. It sees all things in their relationship to the human soul and uses many common words in a deeper sense than we ordinarily use them. For example, the word bread in the Bible means, not just any kind of physical food, which is the broadest interpretation that is put upon it in general literature, but "all the things that man requires;" all physical things, such as clothing, shelter, money, education, companionship etc. And above all, it stands for spiritual things such as realization. Examples – "Give us this day our daily bread." "I am the bread of life." "Unless you eat this bread."

Another example is the word "prosperity". In the biblical sense, "prosperity" and "prosper" signify much more than acquiring material things. They really mean success in prayer. If our prayers are successful, we will naturally have all of the material things that we need.

To be "poor in spirit" does not in the least mean "poor spirited" or "down in spirit." To be "poor in spirit" means to have emptied yourself of all desire to experience personal self will and to have renounced all preconceived opinions in a wholehearted search for God. It means to be willing to set aside present habits of thought, everything that can stand in the way of finding and connecting to God. It means to always be cognizant of the need for God. One of my now deceased congregants used to put it this way, "I can't get enough of this wonderful stuff." So we, too, must always stay in a posture of looking to receive more spiritually. We must be willing to submit, surrender and be obedient to God. God must be always recognized and acknowledged as our source.

Beatitude 2: "Blessed *are* they that mourn: for they shall be comforted."

Mourning, suffering and sorrow are not, in and of themselves, a good thing. Neither is it the will of God, for the will of God is that everyone experience happiness and joyous success. In John 10:10 Jesus says, "I am come that they might have life and that they might have it more abundantly."

Nevertheless, pain, trouble and suffering are extremely useful because many of us will not bother to learn Spiritual Truth until driven to do so by sorrow and failure. Sorrow then becomes a relatively good thing. Many of us will not undertake the search for God wholeheartedly unless driven by trouble of some kind. There is really no need for man to have trouble, because if he would only seek God first, the trouble need never come.

We always have the choice of learning by spiritual unfoldment or learning by painful experience. When we learn by spiritual unfoldment, we follow the first Beatitude and remain poor in spirit.

As a rule, only when health is broken down, and ordinary medical means fail do we seriously look for spiritual help and direction. We must ultimately acknowledge God as our true source if we are to prosper physically, mentally, and spiritually. Some of us just will not seek God until we hit "rock bottom".

This general principle applies to every one of our difficulties, not just financial or physical troubles, but family troubles, quarrels and alienations; and everything else that afflicts us.

They never need to come if we seek first the Kingdom of God. But if we do not seek God, then the suffering must come. For us, this mourning will be a blessing in disguise, for through it we will be comforted. There is an equivalent blessing for every trial we go through. Romans 5:3 says, "But we glory in tribulations also: knowing that tribulation worketh patience." Mourning in this sense does not mean lamenting the loss of some loved one, but the pain and anguish that come when our lives are not aligned with God.

"Pain is the universal language understood and respected by all," says Napoleon Hill in his classic book, *You Can Work Your Own Miracles*. It is the means that forces us to observe the law of self-preservation. When you get a headache, it makes you seek relief to preserve self.

Along with the universal language of pain, God provides us with the means to endure pain. Most pain, both physical and mental, is greatly exaggerated by one's mental reaction to it. Mastering pain provides us unexcelled opportunity to take full possession of our mind, the starting point for all results, effects, and circumstances in life.

The mastery of pain strongly indicates that one has taken complete charge of his own mind, this being the one thing, and the only thing over which God provided man with the privilege of absolute control.

In practicing this, "Be – Attitude" or "Right – Attitude" you begin to "live" your religion rather than just accepting it as something to "believe". Mourning and sorrow gives you the opportunity to discover the greatness of your own mind (the God within you).

Suffering through physical or mental "mourning" – frustrations, sorrows, and disappointments–is the means by which one may become great or go down in permanent failure. The determining factor, as to which of these two circumstances one embraces, depends entirely upon one's mental attitude toward them. Mourning can be either a "stumbling block" or a "stepping stone". Always remember that God maintains a balance in all things and never permits one to suffer any form of hurt or discomfort without providing a means of its cure. "There hath no temptation taken you but such as is common to man: but God is faithful who will not suffer you to be tempted above that ye are able; but will with the temptation also make a way to escape, that ye may be able to bear it" (I Corinthians10:13).

Beatitude 3: "Blessed *are* the meek: for they shall inherit the earth."

On the surface, this Beatitude seems to contradict the everyday facts of life. It is for this reason that sensible people who are being abused, mistreated, and oppressed simply cannot accept the fact that if they just continue to suffer such abuse in silence, that they will inherit the earth. This is, as a matter of fact, exactly the way that our slave oppressors intended for us to interpret this passage. The slave masters read to us from Bunyan's *Pilgrim's Progress* (according to Edward Blyden's research) and had us to believe that if we suffer on earth, we will receive our reward in heaven. No sensible person in looking at the world or studying history can sincerely accept this saying at its face value. But, we cannot evade or discard this text.

What did Jesus Mean?

Jesus either meant what He said, or He did not; and either He knew what he was talking about, or He did not. Either Jesus is a reliable guide or He is not. If He is a reliable guide, He meant what He said, and He has the best approach to our living artful, productive, and divine lives.

When we really understand the truth that Jesus taught we would find it to be not only practical, but also very powerful. Jesus did not deal in empty platitudes. This particular Beatitude is one of the most important verses in the Bible.

When you really possess the spiritual meaning of this text, you have the Secret of Dominion, Rulership and Authority. It will give you the secret of overcoming every kind of difficulty. This Beatitude is the message of Jesus reduced to one sentence.

There are two anchor words in this verse "meek" and "earth". Both of these words have deep spiritual meaning which must be unveiled before their powerful meaning can be grasped.

First of all, the word earth does not, in the Bible, mean just the physical earth. It really means "manifestation." Manifestation is the result of a cause. Now we have learned in previous lessons that our mind is the cause of everything that happens in our bodies and in the affairs of our lives, our homes, and our business; as all that we experience is but the manifestation of our own mental states. It does not matter that you are not consciously aware of it, but in your subconscious mind your thoughts translate into material, physical reality.

In other words, your "earth" means your entire outer experience, and to "inherit the earth" means to have power or dominion over your outer experience; that is, to have power to bring harmony and true success into your life. The Bible says, "All the Earth shall be filled with the glory of the Lord." His soul shall dwell at ease, and his seed (prayers) shall inherit the earth. The Lord reigneth, let the earth rejoice" (Psalm 96:9-13). So we see that when the Bible talks about the earth – possessing the earth, governing the earth, making the earth glorious and so forth, it is referring to the conditions of our lives from our bodily health outwards to the farthest point in our affairs. So this verse tells us how we can possess, or govern, to be masters of our lives and destiny.

How is this Done?

This Beatitude says that dominion, or power over the conditions of our lives, is to be obtained in a certain way by "meekness." But the word "meekness" also has a special meaning. Its true significance is not at all the meaning the word now has in English. In modern times the word "meek" suggests a cowardly person, lacking in courage and self-respect, of no use to himself or anyone else, crawling like a worm. With this view of "meekness" when we come to this passage we find it almost impossible to accept. To the downtrodden, it is well known Frederick Douglas said, – "Power concedes nothing."

In the New Testament Greek the word meek is "prautes" which is not an outward behavior of natural disposition or in relations with his fellowman, but mainly toward God. According to Aristole this word prautes is the type of anger between orgulotes which means "angry without reason" and aorgesia which means "not getting angry at all". Meek, in this sense, is "gentleness in power" that is, getting angry at the right time, with the right measure, and for the right reason. It is strict discipline of the mind.

In Ghana, West Africa, there is an Akan symbol of a ruler or king holding an egg in his hand that adequately expresses the meaning of this Beatitude. The ruler must hold the egg, representative of his power, just right. He must hold the egg firmly enough so as not to drop it, and gently enough so as not to crush it.

The true significance of the word "meek" in the Bible is a mental attitude of open-mindedness; faith in God and the realization that God's will for us is always positive, joyous and better than anything we could think of for ourselves. Such a mental attitude is the secret of "prosperity" and success in life.

This state of mind includes a willingness to allow the will of God to come about in whatever way the Creator considers being best. To inherit the earth, we must absolutely acquire this meekness.

We must understand that to conform to the will of God, rather than losing something means that we gain a better life.

There is an Oriental saying that "Meekness compels God Himself". "Will a child ask his father for bread and he give him a stone?" (Matthew 7:9) This question by Jesus covers the compelling nature of God's response to man. If we submit to God totally, we will be successful as we are open to his direction for our lives.

Beatitude 4: "Blessed *are* they which do hunger and thirst after righteousness: for they shall be filled."

"Righteousness," like the words "meek" and "earth," has a very special spiritual meaning in this Beatitude.

It means in the Bible, not just right conduct, but right thinking in all aspects of life. As we study the Sermon on the Mount, it reiterates over and over the truth that outside things are nothing but the expression or out-picturing of our inner thoughts and beliefs, and that we can make or mar our lives by the way we think. Jesus tells us that these outer things are the results or consequences of what goes on in our minds.

This is the great law of life – that what you think in your mind you will produce in your experience. "As within, so without." You cannot think one thing and produce something else. If you want health, you must first think health. But you must also remember that thinking health does not just mean thinking a healthy body, as important as that is, but it also means thinking peace, and contentment, and goodwill to all, because we already know that destructive emotion is one of the primary causes of disease. If you want spiritual growth and development in the knowledge of God, you must think spiritual thoughts – God thoughts – and give your attention, which is your life, to God, rather than to limitation.

If you want financial success, you must first think prosperous thoughts and make a habit of doing so. "Like begets like" means that as a man soweth in his unseen thoughts, so shall he reap in that which is seen.

Righteousness, then, is the thinking of harmonious thoughts. This principle is simple, but to do so is not easy. Why? Because of the power of habit, and habits (*thinking* in a routinized way) are very hard to break. It is a lot easier to break physical habits than thinking habits because action on the physical level is slower. Our thoughts, on the other hand, are very rapid. Your mind can move from past to present or future with equal ease. You cannot destroy the "old Adam," as Paul says, in a very short time. But, however long it takes, you must continue to accentuate the positive, and it will eliminate the negative. Don't dwell on your mistakes or the slowness of progress, but claim the presence of God within you. Claim power and claim wisdom.

Take inventory of your life and see if you are not still thinking wrongly in some section of your mind. Is there some negative behavior you are still pursuing? Is there somebody you have not forgiven? Are you engaging in any kind of racial, religious, or political hatred? Be careful! Such things can hide easily under the cloak of self-righteousness. Is there some type of jealousy in your heart? Is there some remorse you are holding onto about past mistakes? To revel in remorse is contrary to an understanding of the forgiveness of God. It is divinely ordained and spiritual law that any wholehearted search and quest for truth and righteousness, if persevered in, will be crowned with success.

In this Beatitude Jesus tells us not to be discouraged because we don't overcome everything at once. But if we are moving, if things are improving, though slowly, we should be encouraged. We must just keep working, keep putting forth supreme effort; that is to say, "hungering" and "thirsting" after righteousness and ultimately we shall surely be filled.

Beatitude 5: "Blessed *are* the merciful: for they shall obtain mercy."

These words in this Beatitude, unlike the previous ones, carry the ordinary meaning we still give them in daily life. It again, though, applies to our thought. We must be merciful in thought. Kind actions coupled with unkind thoughts are hypocrisy. They are counterfeits and they bless neither the giver nor the recipient. On the other hand, true thought about others blesses them spiritually, mentally and materially;

and blesses us too. The more somebody errs, the more urgent is the need for us to help them to get free. This is the responsibility the spiritual person has. The true point the Christian needs to grasp is, again, the power of our thoughts. We must be merciful in our thought. Some of us can act kindly, but carry unkind thoughts; that is hypocrisy.

The fact is that as you are merciful to others you, yourself, will ultimately receive the same treatment you give to others. In your hour of need, you will receive the same merciful help from those who are farther along the path than you are. As well, as you don't condemn others, it will free you from condemnation by others. We must be merciful in our mental judgment of others. Because you understand the power of Spirit, you have a responsibility that you must not evade.

Beatitude 6: "Blessed *are* the pure in heart: for they shall see God."

Again the words in this verse have a spiritual meaning. Look at the promise in this Beatitude first. The promise is to see God. Now we know that God has no physical form and, therefore, there is no question of "seeing" Him in the ordinary physical sense. What the verse speaks of is "spiritual perception," and spiritual perception means just the capacity to understand the nature of being. In the realm of the Spirit, there is no limitation. We must overcome our sense of limitation and see God as He really is. If we could see God physically, God would be limited and therefore, not be God. God is all around us, but because we lack spiritual perception, we are unable to recognize the fact that God *is* all around us.

How Do We Do This?

To "see God" is to understand Truth as it really is. We must be "pure in heart." Purity is recognizing God, alone, as the only real power in existence. We must recognize God as the only real cause in every aspect of our lives. We must keep nothing back from God and bring our own will into harmony with God's will.

We must, when we become "pure in heart," recognize God as the only real power, the only real presence in every part of our lives.

The word heart in the Bible usually means that part of man's mentality which modern psychology calls the "subconscious mind". Unless a truth is accepted in the subconscious mind and put into our entire mentality, it cannot make any difference in our character or life. We cannot just accept a truth with the conscious mind only. At the conscious level it is just an opinion. We must internalize into our entire mentality any truth that is to make a difference in our lives.

Most of us have knowledge (degrees etc.) that does not affect or improve our lives. We need besides "head knowledge," "heart knowledge." Medical people know all about health, but can sometimes be the most unhealthy people. Some educators are acquainted with the accumulated wisdom of the ages, but do very stupid things in their personal lives. We must be "pure in heart". Many oppressed individuals having received negative indoctrination, about who they are and what they cannot do from "authority figures," have limitations placed on their expectations of themselves. To truly "see God" is to know that God has unlimited power and that as beings in His likeness that we have unlimited potential. Because God is Spirit, we must rid our spirits of any emotional blocks that prevent our connection to God. When our spirits are clear of hatred, fear, guilt, and feelings of inferiority, we have "pure hearts" (minds) and we can then see the reality of the unlimited power of God.

Beatitude 7: "Blessed *are* the peacemakers: for they shall be called the children of God."

This Beatitude gives us a lesson in the art of "Prayer." Prayer changes things! You cannot pray without some degree of change. Prayer ushers you into the presence of God. And the presence of God changes your outlook. Prayer involves any type of communion with God. This is not just a pretentious platitude. The peacemakers referred to here are those who develop peace in their own minds and spirits – who surmount limitation and become actually, not potentially, the children of God. This condition of mind is the objective that Jesus gives instructions for in the Sermon on the Mount.

Serenity or peace is the passport to the presence of God. The great essential for success in prayer, which is communion with God, is that we first attain some degree of true peace of mind. As long as there is fear, or resentment, or any trouble in your heart; that is to say, as long as you lack serenity, or peace, it is not for you to attain very much. You must have inner peace to be able to focus and concentrate. Some degree of peace is essential to the attainment of true concentration.

Now peacemaker in the usual sense of litigating fights and arguments is laudable; but it hardly ever works. Getting into other people's strife often makes things worse. Personal opinion will often leak in and that opinion will sometimes be wrong. You may well fill a pothole temporarily, when what you really need is a new road altogether. You may get a compromise, but no true peace, because both adversaries are not satisfied and forgiving.

But once the power of prayer is understood, you will be able to really heal quarrels in a true way. There is power and wisdom in God which can cause trouble to melt away almost imperceptibly.

Beatitude 8: "Blessed *are* they which are persecuted for righteousness' sake: for theirs is the kingdom of heaven. Blessed are ye, when *men* shall revile you, and persecute *you*, and shall say all manner of evil against you falsely, for my sake. Rejoice and be exceeding glad: for great is your reward in heaven: for so persecuted they the prophets which were before you."

In light of our knowledge that God wills that we have harmony, joy and peace which we can have through cultivating right thoughts or "righteousness," this statement seems to be a paradox. Here we are told it is blessed to be persecuted as a result of our right thinking or "righteousness;" that it is cause for rejoicing and gladness to be reviled and accused.

All of this is startling, but correct. But we have to understand that the source of all this persecution is none other than our own selves. When we find right thinking or righteousness very difficult – when we are tempted to hold wrong thoughts about some situation, or some person, or about ourselves; to give way to fear, or anger, or despondency – then we are being persecuted for righteousness' sake. This is a war between the higher or spiritual self and the lower or human self. All of the prophets became victorious by overcoming their psycho-spiritual anguish. The old Adam or their lower natures were persecuting them. Jesus, Himself, the Bible states, "was tempted in all respects as we are." He had to meet this persecution more than once. He met it in the Garden of Gethsemane and on the Cross. Since the battles with our lower self must be fought, the sooner we fight them, the better, and so relatively speaking they are great blessings.

Note that there is no virtue or advantage whatsoever in being persecuted by other people. Self-righteous, vain people, when they feel they have been mistreated, are often inclined to claim that they are being "persecuted" on account of their spiritual superiority, and give themselves absurd airs on this ground. This is a pathetic fallacy. Such persons develop a "holy martyr" complex.

There is no virtue in martyrdom. Jesus was not a "martyr." He could have saved Himself if He wished to avoid the crucifixion. He deliberately chose to do a certain work for us in His own way; it was necessary that He die to triumph over death.

Don't fix yourself on martyrdom, or you will ultimately bring it to you. Remember – "As a man thinketh in his heart so is he."

Every spiritual journey involves a struggle with our lower self. Your mental state determines the outcome of your physical existence. If you allow your lower emotions to overtake your higher self, these lower emotions will guide you straight into persecution. But, if you nurture and feed your higher self, you will be victorious and you will experience a heaven (state of mind) and heaven (experience) in your life.

The Kingdom of God The Hidden Power Within

Chapter VI

The words "know thyself," as Lionel Stebbing writes in *A Dictionary of Occult Science*, "summarize the path which leads to insight and to clear knowledge of the Spiritual world." "Know thyself" does not mean become introspective, but know how you are related to the cosmic worlds.

The divine exercise of self-knowledge, which ultimately enables man to live in happiness and in harmony with the divine laws of God, is based primarily on a careful study of the special relationship existing between man and the universe (nature). Man is, as Stebbing puts it, "the impression of the cosmos, its seal and image, and is in body, soul and spirit a miniature cosmos." Man is a microcosm reflecting the macrocosm. That is to say, as God created the entire universe of one essence, man has within him all of the elements found in the universe. Man has within him iron, magnesium, calcium, and electromagnetic energy; that is, everything found in the cosmos.

Man, thus, can be regarded as a little universe in himself, reflecting in a small way the workings of the universe. Hence, the true knowledge of man leads to "the Universe of the stars and the Universe of the atoms" and vice versa. The statement "know thyself" was a Spiritual exhortation to know everything in the world and its relationship to man so as to have true insight into the purpose and power of his earthly existence.

Psalm 19 relates that the universe ("the heavens") tells us the "glory" (majestic secrets) of God; that the universe talks to us ("day upon day it uttereth speech") and reveals divine wisdom to all of us if we are spiritually conscious:

> The heavens declare the glory of God; the skies proclaim the work of His hands day after day they pour forth speech; night after night they display knowledge. There is no speech or language where their voice is not heard. Their voice goes out into all the earth and, their words to the ends of the world (NIV).

In other words, nature talks and in talking reveals the wisdom of God. The study of nature (the universe) and knowledge of the unity and interaction between man and the universe can be the source of the greatest power to man. George Washington Carver demonstrated the fact that such knowledge can take man to heights seemingly unbelievable. Carver was much more than a saintly scientist with a peculiar interest in peanuts. He was a student of God and of his universe as John Ferrell states in his book, *Fruits of Creations– A Look at Global Sustainability As Seen Through The Eyes of George Washington Carver:* "and he saw that each part of the created world was connected to all others and that everything God made had its message."

As a frail, little, orphaned Black boy he was called the "plant doctor" because of his very early ability to heal sick plants and prescribe for them. He was an extremely spiritual man and when he went to Tuskegee Institute in 1897 he started a Sunday evening Bible study class which he taught for thirty years. One participant commented on his "remarkable" teaching method noting that "he brings the Bible characters home to the students by impersonating them, and shows conclusively that there is no possible conflict between science and the Bible."

He believed that people learned best by beginning with something they already knew, then proceeding to the nearest related unknown. To Carver, education was "understanding relations."

When asked how he healed plants, he said that he observed them, talked to them, and then prayed and it was revealed to him what their sickness was and also the cure. As regards to his having made over 200 products from peanuts, he said he took a handful of peanuts and looked at them. He then asked God, – "Great Creator, why did you make the peanut? Why?" He stated that … "all my life I have risen regularly at four o'clock and have gone into the woods and talked with God. There he gives me my orders for the day." He called his laboratory "God's Little Workshop" and often quoted scriptural passages that he believed had relevance to his thought and works. And when asked "What, Dr. Carver, is the most marvelous fact of the age, or the ages, the most wonderful conception of your mind?" His answer was: "the creation story, the creation of the world."

> In the beginning God created the heavens and the earth.. And God said, "Behold, I have given you every herb yielding seed, which is upon the face of all the earth, and every tree, in which is the fruit of a tree yielding seed; to you it shall be for food." (Genesis 1:29)
>
> "Behold," He said means "look," "search," and "find out". That, to me, is the most wonderful thing of life.

> To me, nature in its varied forms is the little windows through which God permits me to commune with Him, and to see much of His glory, by simply lifting the curtain and looking in.

In one particular speech given in 1924, he asserted that "no books ever go into my laboratory. I never have to grope for methods; the method is revealed at the moment I am inspired to create something new. Without God to draw aside the curtain, I would be helpless." A *New York Times* writer found his speech deplorable. "Real chemists, or at any rate, other real chemists," said the writer, "do not scorn books... and they do not ascribe their successes, if they have any, to inspiration." In two separate responses to this ridicule he first stated that, "I regret exceedingly that such a gross misunderstanding should arise as to what I meant by divine inspiration. Inspiration is never at variance with information; in fact, the more information one has, the greater will be the inspiration."

Later he responded in *The Golden Age, a* Jehovah's Witness magazine:

> I know that my redeemer liveth. I know the source from whence my help comes. Inspiration means simply God speaking to man through the things He has created; permitting him to interpret correctly the purposes the Creator had in permitting them to come into existence.

He disavowed any suggestion that he was a genius. When great institutions like MIT, Harvard, and Yale asked him to come teach at their schools, he rejected their offers in order to remain at Tuskegee. He told his students there that he was no genius, but that if they studied God's word, prayed, and observed nature that they would be able to manifest the same power that he had exhibited in his work.

The special teachings about tapping the divine power of God in man in ancient times was confined to the mystery schools and was known or referred to as "entering the Kingdom of God." Such knowledge was revealed only to a few specially selected people called "initiates". The revealed secrets of nature – physical, psychic, mental, and spiritual – helped to develop the hidden powers of man and gave the initiate great advantage over his ignorant fellowman.

This ancient science of "knowing self" consisted of "esoteric" or secret teachings and "exoteric" or outward, public knowledge. The Heriophants of ancient Egypt, the initiated Brahmins of ancient India and later the Hebrew rabbis all preserved their secret beliefs, fearing that they would be profaned. The initiates of every country guarded such secrets very strictly and it is known that none of the ancient nations taught the masses its occult secrets.

Today, we have lost much of this ancient knowledge as a result of the wholesale destruction of the earliest records of mankind that existed in the great libraries of ancient times and other places of learning such as monasteries.

Some of the powers of the Egyptian initiates, for example, were said to have been television without machinery; the ability to transport one's astral self to any distance at will; the power of healing; and that of levitation without trance. The original masons who built the pyramids were said to have possessed the secrets of levitation which were lost before the Middle Ages. The science of levitation was thus applied to lift materials to any height in building the pyramids, as no cranes and no scaffolding were used then.

It is reported that Japanese scientists and engineers, with all of their advanced technology, went to Egypt recently to attempt to erect a pyramid but, after several futile attempts gave up. David Lewis shares valuable pertinent information on the history of the pyramids in his book, *Mysteries of the Pyramids.*

> The Great Pyramid of Gizeh is one example of the great esoteric knowledge possessed by the ancient Egyptians. It is the most perfectly oriented structure in the world. It is situated due north and south, varying only 5 solar seconds, or 3/16 of an inch from being at the precise center of all of the earth's land mass – meaning there is equal land to its north, south, east, and west. This accurate geographic location is significant because it determined our present calendar days and years.

When it was constructed many thousands of years ago, 2144 BC (some 2,140 years before the birth of Christ), its outer casing had a marble smooth surface that served as a reflection of light, indicating the solstices of winter and summer, and spring and autumn equinoxes.

The name "pyramid" is from the Greek <u>pyramidos</u> the Hebrew derivative being <u>Urimmidin</u>. <u>Urim</u> means "light" or "revelation" and <u>middin</u> means "measures," therefore denoting a revelation in measures.

The structure is 13 square acres, 762 feet square, 486 feet high, with each stone weighing 5 to 30 tons each. It is constructed of over 2 million blocks weighing more than 75 million tons.

European "scho (liars)" theorize that about 200,000 slaves built the pyramid rolling the 3-5 ton blocks on logs over a 40 mile distance. However, to roll blocks that size over a 40 mile distance through deep sand, over water, and sand dunes is virtually impossible. Secondly, the surrounding lands of Egypt had no great oak trees – only reed-like palm trees which do not make a roller. As well, a line of the number of slaves pulling such blocks by rope over log rollers would form a line extending 10 to 14 miles across the desert flats, and the pulling power would decrease with each mile.

Further, no scaffold could have been erected having the ability to bear the weight of those blocks. These blocks, 5-30 tons each, were cut to precise accuracy and lifted into place and laid on a mortar base less than 1/8 inch thick. If the blocks had been slid into position, the motion of the sliding block would have removed the mortar.

The pyramids were built by accessing the hidden powers of God that reside in man – the Kingdom of God.

Jesus and Esoteric Knowledge

The Bible is full of references to secret, spiritual knowledge – full of references to the secret, psychic, spiritual sciences. In the Old Testament we learn of Abraham, Issac, Jacob, and Moses who were remarkable mediums through whom Jehovah God offered divine guidance.

The psychic picture painted for us in the New Testament is similar and is centered on Jesus, whose inspiration came from His heavenly Father. In fact Jesus was a living person of divine origin.

We emphasize, at this point, that when Herod decreed that all male Hebrew boys born in Rome be killed, Jesus' parents escaped to Egypt with Him (Matthew 2:13).

Levi H. Dowling, a pioneer preacher in the Disciples of Christ denomination, U.S. Army medical chaplain, medical doctor, and literary writer had a vision while just a small child. His vision was to build the "White City" which he later came to know was to be his book titled *The Aquarian Gospel of Jesus Christ,* which was first published in 1908. He reports that his revelations about Jesus came through the "Akashic Records," of Sankrit origin meaning "primary substance". He stated that this primary substance is really universal mind that any man can enter once he comes into a certain spiritual consciousness.

Thusly, in section XI, entitled *Life and Works of Jesus in Egypt* chapter 47 he records:

> Jesus with Elihu and Salome in Egypt tells the story of his journeys. Elihu and Salome praised God. Jesus goes to the temple in

> Heliopolis and is received as a pupil.
>
> And Jesus stayed in Zoan many days and then went forth unto the city of the sun, that men call Heliopolis, and sought admission to the temple of the sacred brotherhood. (Verse 9).
>
> The master said, take the vow of secret brotherhood. *And Jesus took the vow of secret brotherhood. (underlined for emphasis by the author). (Verse 15).*

An accepted psychic in the spiritual context, Edgar Cayce, also had some interesting remarks about Jesus' possible exposure to the mystery (psychic) schools. Cayce, in the course of his years as a trance medium, exhibited thousands of verifiable diagnoses and cures for people thousands of miles away. He was an ardent, almost fanatical Baptist, and was shocked upon first awakening from a trance to hear he had spoken of Jesus' travelling and studying in foreign lands in the East. He later became convinced that it was true.

Professor James in his work, *Stolen Legacy,* states, "all the great religious leaders from Moses to Christ were initiates of the Egyptian Mysteries." Lawrence E. Carter in his book, *Nile Valley Civilizations,* states that, "according to Dr. Martin Bernal of Cornell University, the Greeks and Romans believed that their religion came from Egypt. It is more accurate to view Christianity as a Judeo-Egyptian religion rather than a Judeo-Grecian religion."

Count C. F. Volney, noted and respected French scholar of the late 1700s, wrote in his book, *Ruins of Empires*, that, "All religions originated in Africa. We are indebted to the ancient Ethiopians for various religious systems now so highly revered by the different branches of both the Semitic and Aryan races."

As to the strong possibility that Jesus studied in the ancient mystery temples of Egypt, fascinating stories from the research of Janet Bock in her book, *The Jesus Mystery – of Lost Years and Unknown Travels,* deserve our attention. Her search for the "lost years of Jesus (between ages 12 and 30) not recorded in the Canon was prompted by Dowling's *Aquarian Gospel.* With that as a catalyst, she began to look for other relevant material and soon heard of a book by a Russian named Nicolas Notovitch who had traveled extensively in India and Tibet in the late 1880s.

She found a copy of the original 1890 edition. In it Notovitch tells a fascinating story of his travels which culminated in an accident where he was thrown from a donkey on a steep mountain that forced him to recuperate at a Buddhist monastery in the western region of Tibet. Notovitch, in his travels, had heard enigmatic tales of a saint from the west revered by the Hindus named Issa, the Buddhist equivalent of the name of Jesus. In the book, *Caesar and Christ*, Will Durant explains that Jesus' parents gave him the quite common name Yesua (our Joshua) meaning "the help of Yahveh;" the Greeks made this into "Jesus," the Romans into "Iesus." Notovitch was shown a manuscript about Issa that not only paralleled what the Bible says about Jesus, but also included his life from ages 12 to 30 as well. Notovitch was told that the original manuscript was located in the great monastery at Lhas, near the capitol of Tibet, with copies in several of the country's major monasteries.

It was related that the original manuscript was written in India and later brought to Tibet. Notovitch's guide translated the verses of the manuscript for him which he later reproduced in his book. His belief in the authenticity of the manuscript prompted him to challenge anyone doubting his work to travel to Tibet to do a mission study of their own to verify its historical value.

No one accepted the invitation until 35 years later. In 1922 Swami Abhedananda went to the Himis and saw the manuscript that Notovich wrote about in his Bengali Book of Travels called *The Unknown Life of Jesus Christ*. Bock, upon reading the verses of what she came to call the "Tibetan Legend of Issa," was struck by the uncanny similarity between the description of Jesus' life published in 1890 and Dowling's *Aquarian Gospel*, first published in 1911. She offers two possible explanations for the similarity. Either Dowling's *Aquarian Gospel* is an amplification of the earlier Notovitch manuscript, without giving credit to the source; or if the Tibetan legend is true, any subsequent telling of the story, whether by ancient manuscript or divine revelation, would be basically the same. The manuscripts relate to us, first of all, according to the accounts given by merchants arriving from Judea in the same year when the death of Jesus occurred, that a just man by the name of Issa, an Israelite, inspite of his being acquitted twice by the judges as being a man of God, was nevertheless put to death by the order of the pagan governor Pilate. Pilate feared that he might take advantage of his great popularity to re-establish the Kingdom of Israel and expel from the country its conquerors. Only at the end of the second volume is found the first categorical affirmation of the chronicler. He says there that, "Issa was a man blessed by

God and the best of all."

The following is a portion of the condensed version of the Legend of Issa published in 1890 by Nicolas Notovitch in his book titled *The Unknown Life of Jesus Christ.*

1. For there was tortured and murdered the great and just Issa, in whom was manifest the soul of the Universe.
2. Which had incarnated in a simple mortal to benefit men and destroy the evil spirit in them.
3. To lead back to peace, love and happiness, man degraded by his sins, and recall him to the one and indivisible Creator whose mercy is infinite.
4. And to show by example how man can attain moral purity and free his soul from the domination of the physical senses, so that it may achieve the perfection necessary for it to enter the Kingdom of Heaven, which is immutable and where bliss eternal reigns.
5. The parents of the infant were poor people.
6. The divine child, to whom the name Issa was given, commenced in his tender years to talk of the only and indivisible God, exhorting the strayed souls to repent from their sins.
7. Then Issa secretly absented himself from his father's house; left Jerusalem, and in a train of merchants, journeyed toward Sindh (ancient name of India) Note: India and Africa at this point in history were all one land mass).
8. He went to Djagguernat where they taught him to read and to understand the Vedas, to cure physical ills by means of prayers, to teach and expound the sacred scriptures, to drive out evil desires from man and make him again in the likeness of God.
9. The White priests and the warriors, who had learned of Issa's discourse to the Sudras (the oppressed) resolved upon his death and sent their servants to find the young teacher and slay him.

All of these references amplify and correspond to the Canonical Scriptures. They indicate, as well, the nature of Jesus; that He was not born "co-substantial" or "co-equal" with God, but attained the Christ nature, the Christ consciousness in the course of His lifetime. This will be a very important factor in determining our ability to be a follower of Jesus.

Jesus' Parables on the Kingdom of God

The name "Christ" corresponds with the Hebrew word "Messias" and means "anointed one" sent from the spiritual world (heaven) to the aid of humanity on earth. The baptism of Jesus by John in the river Jordan, which signified union with the spirit, made it possible for the personality of Jesus to receive into its own soul the Christ, the Logos; so that he became flesh in it. From the time of this incarnation, the Jesus of Nazareth became the Christ and the personality became the bearer of the Logos.

Myles Monroe states that:

> Christ is the image of God. The word image does not mean a "statue of something." It means when God created you, He created you in His image, and His image is Christ... Jesus was the human manifestation of the heavenly Christ. We, as humans on earth, with all our fallibilities and weaknesses – God pronounces on us: "you are the body of Christ." In other words Christ is in us somewhere. Christ is in me. Christ is in you. God knows He is there. His image is there, so God called us Christ.

In order to understand the dictum, "man, know thyself" or the whole concept of the "Kingdom of God," we must examine closer the basis of the teachings of Jesus. Before Jesus, the Jews kept intact their science of the secrets of nature (i.e. the knowledge about the "Kingdom of God") within the mystery schools.

But Jesus, Himself a Jew, had little respect for some of the "narrow" religious practices of His people, their rites and ceremonies etc. Therefore Jesus decided, after his special secret training from the ages 12 to 30, to spread the secret knowledge of "the Kingdom of God" to everybody.

However in conformity with the practice of the times, Jesus Christ during the three years of his ministering, adopted two different methods of spreading the knowledge of the "Kingdom of God". He first taught only His disciples the well-guarded secrets (esoteric sciences) which would enable them to achieve great psychic and spiritual powers. The chosen "12" were thus initiated to become the first Christian mystics. On the other hand, He spoke to the masses openly of spiritual truths in parables and taught them to believe implicitly and have faith. "All these things spake Jesus unto the multitude in parables, and without a parable spake he not unto him" (Matthew 13:34). He further states,"...blessed *are* they that have not seen and *yet* have believed" (John 20:29).

Those "that have not seen" were those who had not been given the secret knowledge of the "the Kingdom of God". To Jesus, an uninitiated person who had this faith would lead a better life than one without it. The means to happiness and success was not to be confined to a few elect, but given to the whole of humanity. Hence, Jesus said this of His mission on earth in Luke 19:10, "The Son of man is come to seek and to save that which was lost." And then, "I am come that they might have life and that they might have it more abundantly" (John 10:10).

Jesus had good reasons for using these two different methods. As explained previously, He could not reveal the secrets to the ordinary people, but only to the selected few – His disciples. He, therefore, said to the chosen twelve:"Give not that which is Holy unto dogs, neither cast ye your pearls before swine, lest they trample them under their feet, and turn again and rend you" (Matthew 7:6).

This simply means that precious things like pearls should not be given to swine which have no use for them. For when they see the pearls are not food, they will become angry and attack the donor – a sure warning against the revelation of the secrets of life to those unprepared for them.

Speaking of his intent to share the mysteries of "the Kingdom of God" with His disciples, on the other hand, He says, "Unto you is given to know the mystery of the Kingdom of God; but unto them that are without, all these things are done in parables (Mark 4:11).

As Geoffrey Hudson explains in *The Hidden Wisdom in the Holy Bible Volume I*, "knowledge is power," and since power in the wrong hands could be dangerous, modern scientists also keep secret knowledge such as atomic power from the masses of people. This is why Jesus told His disciples, after imparting the secrets to them, "Go ye and tell no man," implying both secrecy and silence (Luke 9:21).

With regard to the broad masses, who were to an extent able to share "the knowledge of the kingdom," Jesus devised a simpler method of teaching them to cultivate faith in God and try to find the "Kingdom of God."

To Jesus, the attainment of "the Kingdom of God" was based on development of man from within, development of the human mind to enable it to attract divine power. Put more simply, Jesus' teaching involved drawing from the life-force or energy in the universe, or in Jesus' words "to attain the Kingdom of God." The life-force or energy of God has its contact point in man in the human mind. Man, through his mind, has the ability to indeed function in the image and likeness of God.

To develop the mind in ancient Egypt, riddles were used. Mustafa El-

Amin gives us information on this phenomenon in his book, *Free Masonry, Ancient Egypt and the Islamic Destiny*:

> However, in order to really get into Egypt, it was required that you break or explain the Riddle of the Sphinx. "Entering Egypt" (i.e Entering the Kingdom) didn't mean going there physically. It meant understanding and receiving some of the wisdom and benefits of that great city. Although there were several riddles, one of the most thought-provoking ones was the Riddle of the Sphinx. It was the knowledge of this riddle that was the key to entering Egypt. Why? A close examination of this riddle will reveal that it speaks to the very development and mental progression of man.

According to Tony Browder in his book, *Nile Valley, Contributions to Civilization*, "much of what is known about the Nile Valley mathematics can be found in a document called the *Rhind Mathematical Papyrus*, which was purchased by the Scotsman Alexander Rhind and brought to London.... The text consists of more than 80 mathematical problems and their solutions. One of the more interesting elements of the Rhind Papyrus is problem 79, which deals with a geometric progression of a ratio of 7. It states:

> There are seven houses.
> in each house there are seven cats.
> Each cat kills seven mice.
> each mouse had eaten seven grains.
> Each grain would have produced seven *hekat*.
> What is the sum of all the enumerated elements?

This rhyme is more of a riddle than an algebraic problem because the answer is one.

Adib Rashad in his book, *Ideological Foundation of the Nation of Islam*, indicates that, Master Farad Muhammad, "the enigmatic eclectic savior" of the Nation of Islam drew upon the ancient Egyptian usage of riddles in the 1930s. Rashad says Iman Warith Deen Muhammad points out "that these mathematical lessons were designed to compel the believers to exercise their mental muscles." So without having the believers go to school and learn, these problems (lessons) were forcing the <u>*believers' minds to wake up [the latent power of God that resides in man]*</u> (emphasis by author).

In explaining how to "enter the kingdom of God" Jesus also used riddles to instruct the masses. Given the previous documentation of the high possibility that some of Jesus' "lost years" were spent in Egypt studying the secret knowledge of the hidden power of God that resides in man, we can at least conclude that there is an uncanny similarity between Jesus' method of teaching about the kingdom of God and that of the Egyptian Mystery schools. In all of Jesus' parables about the Kingdom of God, He talked about the hidden power of the mind.

In Matthew 13, there is a series of parables (riddles) about the "Kingdom of God". Now based on the information we have garnered about the definition of the Kingdom of God, let us see if we can decipher their true meaning.

The Parable of the Mustard Seed: *(Matthew 13:31-32) Another parable he put forth unto them, saying the kingdom of heaven is like to a grain of mustard seed, which a man took and sowed in his field, which indeed is the least of all seeds; but when it is grown, it is the greatest among herbs, and becometh a tree, so the birds of the air come and lodge on the branches thereof.* A mustard seed is like the belief of the mind. Faith seems to be a small thing says Jesus, but if you just plant (an idea) and back it with faith, it will grow (manifest) into something visible, tangible and of monumental proportion. The mustard seed is so small as to be invisible but grows to be a giant tree, the boughs of which birds nest in. This is the same way that an idea in the mind backed by faith will manifest as a great physical, material reality.

The Parable of the Yeast: *(Matthew 13:33) Another parable spake he unto them; The kingdom of heaven is like unto leaven, which a woman took, and hid in three measures of meal, till the whole was leavened.* Once again Jesus speaks of an invisible presence; both the seed in the previous parable and yeast are virtually invisible to the eye. The "Kingdom of God" is like yeast. Again belief is invisible but very powerful. Something great is ultimately materialized out of the hidden (invisible) power of belief held in the mind. Just as yeast makes bread rise, so then does faith "blow things up" and again out of something invisible and seemingly small (yeast) comes a great amount of doughbread.

The Parable of A Hidden Treasure in a Field: *(Matthew 13:44): Again, the kingdom of heaven is like unto treasure hid in a field; the which when a man hath found, he hideth, and for the joy thereof goeth and selleth all that he hath, and buyeth that field.* Here Jesus talks about the value of what we think and believe. It is a hidden treasure, that once we discover it, we recognize it as the most powerful and potent possession we have. This parable amplifies the fact that the mind is the true source of everything. The mind is the one and only thing over which we have been given personal control. It is a great, great treasure because everything in the physical/material realm begins as an idea in the mind. Your mind is great and invaluable.

The Pearl: *(Matthew 13:45-46) Again, the kingdom of heaven is like unto a merchant man, seeking goodly pearls: Who, when he had found one pearl of great price, went and sold all that he had, and bought it.* Again Jesus speaks of the tremendous value of belief, of the thought in our minds. The mind, Jesus notes, is like a very valuable pearl. Once you find out the power in the mind you recognize it as the most valuable thing you possess. You hold nothing else as more valuable because nothing else is more valuable.

Dr. Howard Thurman states in his book, *Jesus and the Disinherited*, that in order to truly understand the teachings of Jesus we must understand the "psychological climate [in which Jesus did] his teaching and ministry."

He further states:

> His words were directed to the House of Israel, a minority within the Greco-Roman world smarting under the loss of status, freedom and autonomy and haunted by the dream of the restoration of a lost glory and a former greatness. His message focused on the urgency of a radical change in the inner attitude of the people. He recognized fully that out of the heart are the issues of life and that no external force, however great and overwhelming, can at long last destroy a people if it does not first win the victory of the spirit against them. The basic fact is that Christianity, as it was born in the mind of this Jewish teacher and thinker, appears as a technique of survival for the oppressed. That it became, through the intervening years, a religion of the powerful and the dominant, used sometimes as an instrument of oppression, must not tempt us into believing that it was thus in the mind and life of Jesus.

Thurman's words seem to reflect the thinking of many oppressed people today rather than in the 1940s as he continues:

> I belong to a generation that finds very little that is meaningful

> or intelligent in the teachings of the church concerning Jesus Christ. It is a generation largely in revolt because of the general impression that Christianity is essentially an other-worldly religion, having as its motto: "take all the world, but give me Jesus." The desperate opposition to Christianity rests in the fact that it seems, in the last analysis, to be a betrayal of the Negro into the hands of his enemies by focusing his attention upon heaven, forgiveness, love and the like.... Living in a climate of deep insecurity, Jesus, faced with so narrow a margin of civil guarantees, [He] had to find some other basis upon which to establish a sense of well-being. He knew that the goals of religion, as he understood them, could never be worked out within the then established order. Deep from within that order he projected a dream, the logic of which would give to all the needful, security.... The Kingdom of God is Within!! The basic principles of His way of life cut straight through the despair of his fellows and found it groundless.

Thurman concludes "that by inference," Jesus says:

1. You must abandon your fear and fear only God.
2. You must not indulge in any deception or dishonesty even to save your lives.

Entering the Kingdom of God How The Mind Works

Chapter VII

Since Jesus' answer to the plight of an oppressed minority in the midst of a repressive environment was to enter the "Kingdom of God within," we must understand how this power operates and how we "enter" the Kingdom of God. As well, since ancient Kamit (Egypt) is where the origin of the concept of "entering the Kingdom of God" began, we need to look closer at this idea from its earliest perspective.

To "know thyself" in the earliest concept of the Kingdom of God, meant to awaken the hidden power of (God) that resides in man.

A study of Kamitic religion will show that religion is a system designed to help man reunite him/herself with God, through the essential qualities that they both share. So then what is Man? David raises this question in Psalm 8. He says that when he "consider(s)" the meticulous, careful precision with which God has made all of the rest of his creation (the moon, stars, heavens, etc.) and that God has given man "dominion" over all of that, he concludes man must really be something extraordinary. He then goes on to describe man as the supreme being (God) over all of God's other creation.

So then man is mind (the essence of God) and he must understand how his mind works to then effectively use it for his own well-being.

The crucial question to be asked at this point is whether man has the capacity, the equipment, or the power to control his life; whether he can be what he wants to be. This is a crucial question for the oppressed and particularly in the context of what Jesus' message says to the downtrodden.

Millions of dispossessed, disenfranchised individuals are affected by unemployment, poverty, broken homes, alcohol and substance abuse, and crime. Millions of others suffer physical, mental and spiritual disorder in countless forms. The plethora of problems affecting and afflicting the masses of impoverished people gives rise to the belief that they are victims of circumstances over which they have no control. Such belief has made many addicts of fatalism, instead of masters and controllers of their destinies.

Such fatalistic belief is contagious, and when individuals submit to its influence, believing that the circumstance around them is stronger than the power within them, such persons are defeated, before they start.

There is an amazing world of power, possibility, and promise available to us, but we must "enter the Kingdom of God" to access it.

The Bible in Proverbs 23:7 reveals that the mind is the creative cause of all that transpires in our lives; that the personal and collective conditions of our lives are the result of our actions; that all of our actions are the direct outcome of our ideas; and that we never make a move of any kind until we first form some image or plan in our mind. These ideas are powerful. They are potent. They are the causes – good, bad, or indifferent – of the effects that follow in our lives.

Thus the essence of entering the Kingdom of God is this – when we learn to use our minds constructively, we awaken the hidden power of God that resides in man. This is what Jesus meant when He said to Nicodemus, "You must be born again." You are indeed (born) again when you come into awareness of the power of the mind. Our lives are built entirely on the (thoughts) of our mind. And to know the power of our mind and the fact that we are in control of our destiny through the thoughts that we entertain is truly to be born again. The power of God within us is not deliberately hidden from us, but "hidden" means that we have not previously known that this power exists. It has to be awakened!! God has not hidden it from us, but just as Jesus describes in certain parables in Matthew 13, we must discover or uncover this reality about ourselves.

This is a marvelous inner power that exists within man, and the revelation of such a world enables man to do, to attain, and to achieve anything he desires within the bounds of his nature.

Because the development of man's inner thinking is so critical, is why Jesus states in Matthew 6:33 that we are to "seek first the Kingdom of God!" This creative principle is summarized in Proverbs 23:7 – "As a man thinketh in his heart, so is he." Many cannot accept the statement that all negative consequences in their life are the results of their own beliefs, or their own past thinking crystallized into beliefs. They prefer to blame something or someone else. Others have been programmed to believe that in God's good time all things will eventually work out to their satisfaction. They are planning for a heaven to be gained at some future time, when it is actually a condition and state of mind that can be had now as well as hereafter. In fact, if it is not gained in this life, it will never be had in the life to come.

Modern psychology has conclusively demonstrated that a change of thought must precede every change in the life and in the affairs of man.

This, Jesus taught incessantly as he referred to "entering the Kingdom of God."

How does the mind work? In ancient Kamit (Egypt) there was what was known as the "Tree of Life," a schematic of the subconscious mind. These ancient Kamitians understood that man has one mind with two parts or two levels. They used the schematic to catalogue every aspect of the part of the mind called the subconscious, which is the seat of power of the God presence within man. That man is made in the likeness of God means that the faculties making up man's being are the same that God possesses. Thus the tree of life was used to describe God's faculties and behavior as well as man's. Man, like God, can be seen as embodying the following faculties.

1. Man's original and essential state is spiritual – that is energy.
2. Man has the creative faculty of "word power." The Kamitians called it "Hekau." The ancient Kamitians understood, however, that man like God is one being appearing as many, through the differentiating attributes of physical matter. Man's differentiated physical nature causes an illusion and makes it difficult for him to see that he is one with all, because he identifies himself with the physical body. This foundation of false physical self-consciousness is the fundamental cause of man's problems in life. That he sees himself as a physical, fleshly being *only* is to man's greatest detriment.

From an evolutionary aspect, the "animal nature" of man is the oldest and most primitive part of the brain and therefore exerts the strongest influence on him. You may recall even in the Book of Genesis that God first made man of the "dust of the earth," but man had no real life until God breathed Spirit (Himself) into man (Genesis 2:7). To overcome the animal nature – the African-centered approach is based on the fact that within every man there are intuitive (God given) functions that can be activated to gain guidance for correct functioning and living. For example, rather than seeking to emulate Jesus or some other personality like Martin Luther King, Jr., or Malcolm X, we would rather seek to discover which inner shaping forces are responsible for their attainment, and awaken these within ourselves, that they may guide us in the same manner.

This is exactly the teaching of Jesus and the methodology He employed in discipling others. In fact, this is what a disciple is and it is, according to Dr. Tony Evans in his book, *What Matters Most*, that which is most important to Jesus. He notes:

> After His resurrection from the dead, and just before His ascension back into heaven, Jesus told His disciples [and us] what was uppermost on His mind. His last words on earth are recorded for us in Matthew 28:20. Notice verse 19: "Go therefore and make disciples of all the nations." If Christ's mandate for the church is to make disciples, then His will for us as individual believers is that we would *become* disciples... To be a disciple of Christ means that we become like him. That's why Jesus said in Matthew 10:25: "It is enough for the disciple that he become as his teacher." God's goal is not salvation; that's just the introduction to God's goal. His desire is that those who are saved become disciples.

You recall from a previous chapter that Jesus calls us to follow Him, not worship Him. When He says in John 14:6, "I am the way..." He is not talking about Himself the person but the method, the process or the manner of attaining the spiritual power that He manifested. This would be similar to the way some of us in the African American community might ask someone – "Do you know the way to make a cake?" What is being asked is: Do you know the process, the procedure to be followed or the steps to be taken to make a cake?

Thus, says Evans:

> Discipleship is that developmental process of the local church that progressively brings Christians from spiritual infancy to spiritual maturity so that they are then able to reproduce the process within someone else. The word disciple itself from the New Testament Greek means "learner or student." The disciple follows the teacher, takes in information from the teacher, masters the knowledge given by the teacher and then finally is able to model the skills that have been learned.

To many of us "life is an enigma, a deep mystery, an incomprehensible problem," says Raymond Holliwell. "It appears so, but it is very simple if one holds the key. Mystery is only another name for ignorance. All things are mysteries when they are not understood."

Man is a being of constant growth, who has unlimited potential but his inherent powers must be developed and cultivated. He must first of all come into consciousness (awareness) of the nature of his being – that man is mind and that the mind has two parts.

We have then, as the ancient Kamitians taught in their study of the mind, one mind with two levels or parts. We have a conscious mind – which is our moral, rational, thinking mind, and the subconscious mind— which is able to create according to the nature of our emotions. Because the mind is the basic factor and governing power over the entire life of man, we must be aware of the fact that the progress and success of the individual is largely determined by his ruling mental state. Attention must be given to the predominant mental state of one's mind, for it will regulate the action and direction of all one's forces, faculties, and powers; the sum total of which will inevitably determine many particular experiences and personal fate.

Dr. Joseph Murphy, one of the most profound scholars of ancient northeast Africa and great student of the mind relates the following in his landmark bestseller, *The Power of Your Subconscious Mind:*

> Whatever you claim mentally and feel as true, your subconscious mind will accept and bring forth into your (experience). The only thing necessary for you to do is to get your subconscious mind to accept your idea, and the law of your own subconscious mind will bring forth the health, peace or position you desire; you give the demand or decree, and your subconscious will faithfully reproduce the idea impressed upon it. The law of the mind is this: You will get a reaction or a response from your subconscious mind according to the nature of the thought or idea you hold in your conscious mind.

The ruling state of mind is made up of various mental attitudes which the individual adopts from things, events, and life in general. These mental attitudes are based on one's frame of reference: the sum total of what one has been taught, experienced and been exposed to by one's parents, peers, teachers, preachers etc. If one's attitudes are positive, optimistic and affirming, the predominant mental attitude will correspond and exhibit a highly constructive and positive way of life. If the ruling mental state is upward-bound, that is, aspiring, harmonious, and positive, all forces will be directed in constructive channels. But, if the state of mind is downward in tendency, that is, negative and non-affirming, then almost all energy will be misdirected. This is the unfortunate plight of many oppressed individuals. It is obviously evident then, that of all the factors that regulate the life and experience of man, none exercises a greater influence than the ruling state of one's mind.

Thought is a subtle element, although it is invisible to the physical sight, it is an actual force or substance, as real as electricity, light, heat, or water. Scientists relate that thought is compared with the speed of light. They tell us our thoughts travel at the rate of 186,000 miles per second. Our thought travels 930,000 times faster than our voice. No other force in the universe, yet known, is as quick or as great as the mind. It is an unlimited power; your power to think is inexhaustible, and yet few of us are aware of its awesome power. Thusly, whatever we habitually think (ruling state of mind) sinks down into our subconscious mind where the power of God resides in us and then creates, according to the nature of our emotions.

The powers of the subconscious mind are said to be limitless and James T. Mangan in his fascinating book, *The Secret of Perfect Living,* lists them as follows:

> That subconscious in you is powerful!
> It can make a million dollars.
> It can smoke twenty cigars a day.
> It can work a month without sleep.
> It can stop you from doing even five minutes of concentrated work.
> It can make you seriously sick.
> It can cure you of illness the doctors might call incurable.
> It can actually kill you.
> It can save your life.
>
> Properly understood you can work any miracle in the realm of the possible.

So then, whatever we habitually think sinks down into our subconscious mind which then creates according to the nature of our emotions. If we think good, good will follow. If we think evil, evil will follow. This is the way our mind works. My dear sister, Iyanla Vanzant, states that, "where the mind leads, the behind follows." That is to say, whatever circumstances, situations or conditions we find ourselves in, our mind put us there. The main point to remember is that once the subconscious mind accepts an idea, it begins to execute it. This happens not sometimes, but all the time, because this is the law of the mind. At the moment that you are able to contact and realize this law, you will at once begin to enjoy the benefits.

An electrician, for example, does not pray and wait for the electrical energy to make up its mind to serve him. He learns firsthand the laws of conduction and transmission in order to know how to cooperate with the law that governs electrical energy. After gaining this knowledge he can go ahead and set up the machinery which provides the means to generate and direct the power. Then he can put in a switch and just flip it and operate giant machines, set in motion countless other devices, or flood a room with light. He can do this not just once or twice, but as many times as he chooses, so long as he does not violate the law governing the energy. This same principle holds true in all other sciences, including the science of the mind. There is a scientific (right) way of thinking about everything that prevents wasted mental energy and produces the desired result every time.

Again, the main point to remember is that once the subconscious mind accepts an idea, it begins to execute it. And, it all depends on what we believe. This law of belief, when negatively applied is the cause of failure, frustrations, and unhappiness. On the other hand, when your habitual thinking is harmonious and constructive, you experience success, happiness, and prosperity. Whatever you claim mentally and feel as true, your subconscious mind will accept and bring forth into your experience. The only thing necessary for you to do is to get your subconscious to accept your idea as belief. Jesus says it this way: "According to your faith (what you believe) be it unto you" (Matthew 9:29).

When an adverse circumstance arises we are not to come under it, to submit to it as a powerless weakling, but like Jesus told us we are to "...say unto [the] mountain, be thou removed, and be thou cast into the sea" (Mark 11:23).

Dr. Howard Thurman notes that when we "align our minds in oneness with the intent of the mind of God," we cause divine energy to be released. God has good intentions for our lives!! Jesus tells us, "It is your Father's good pleasure to give you the Kingdom" (Luke 12:32). Now since it is God's intention that things go well for us, our intention must take the same direction. Therefore, when our intention becomes reconciled or cooperative with God's intention for us, it calls a force into action which gives direction to the latent power of the mind.

Understanding the power of the "Kingdom within us" and then "entering the Kingdom," we must partner with God by combining and directing all of our thoughts, ideas, and desire for good.

When thoughts come to our subconscious mind, impressions are made on it. Once the subconscious accepts any idea, it moves to put it into effect immediately. When we "desire" something and then "expect" it, we create a line of attractive force. When you desire something and remain constant in that desire, the good demanded is sooner or later realized. The mind is a magnet and attracts whatever corresponds to its ruling state. Whatever we imagine in our mind, whatever we expect and think about will eventually come into our lives. Sometimes it brings about an immediate solution, other times it takes days, weeks, or longer.

An example of an immediate result would be when the former heavyweight champion of the world, Riddick Bowe, won the title from then champion Evander Holyfield. Bowe was training for the fight in Oregon and his trainer, Rock Newman, was not satisfied with his sparring results or his training preparation. Rock called me and asked me if I would come to the camp to work with Bowe. Before I flew out to Oregon I collected tapes of pre-fight interviews and appearances of Muhammad Ali. When I got to Oregon I played the videos for Bowe and asked him to describe what he saw. He repeated the fact that Ali consistently made statements like: "I'm the Greatest!" "I'm Unbeatable!" "Nobody Can Beat Me!" After understanding the dominant belief and thought that Ali had, Bowe was instructed to adopt a similar mental state. The next day he ran longer and faster, destroyed his sparring partners, went on to defeat Evander Holyfield and to become the heavyweight champion of the world.

In another case, I had a member of my congregation who had flunked her Registered Nurse's examination on three separate occasions. But after six weeks in my class on Spiritual Dynamics, she passed the exam with outstanding scores.

When I was growing up as a young boy in Virginia, I saw the power of holding a belief while in a state of trance. If you hold a belief in a state of trance, it gives power to the realization of those beliefs. I saw a man pleading with passersby to help him to remove a 1956 Cadillac weighing over five thousand pounds that had fallen on his son. Naturally, the bystanders, thinking it impossible to lift such a heavy car encouraged the man to wait for a wrecker because they believed it was too heavy for them to move. But at this point of crisis, the father could not wait. Though not stated aloud, in his mind he was making suggestions to his subconscious by saying things like – "I must move this car or my son will die! I *will* move this car." He thus bypassed what his conscious mind would say he could not do and began to make suggestions to his subconscious mind; where the power of God resides in man. By being extremely excited and anxious, he emotionalized his thoughts that served as a catalyst to move his subconscious mind into immediate action. He was then, by himself, able to lift up the front end of this mammoth car while his son was dragged to safety!

In scientific psychological tests, people have been placed in a deep trance (hypnotized) and then given water, but made to believe that they drank vodka instead. Not only did they act inebriated, their vital signs reacted as if they had become inebriated. The opposite experiments conducted with vodka passed as water elicited the same type of response. The subjects, having imbibed enough alcohol to become intoxicated, behaved quite soberly, even down to their vital signs.

The way in which we see images that we entertain in our subconscious mind can have some very serious consequences. The images we see are not just depictions, but they act as funnels that direct the forces of nature to the accomplishment of how we desire certain events to go; as well as condition our spirit to behave as visualized. This is to say that certain automatic responses can be created and reinforced through the images that we entertain.

Therefore, "making images of God in human likeness can be either helpful or dangerous for the follower," says Muata Ashby in his book titled *Egyptian Yoga.* He further states:

> The danger arises when the mind becomes fixed on the image rather than the essence of the symbolic deity to be worshipped. Instead of worshipping those qualities and developing them in one's self, the worshipper might believe that those qualities belong to the statue or painting or are for some special person who lived long ago. They do not realize that the symbols are symbols of the qualities that lie deep within every individual, not somewhere "out there," but "right in here" inside each one of us.

This is why the wise sages of ancient Egypt chose images that were so far from the norm, that the attachment-oriented human mind would not get "hung up" on the "picture" but rather concentrate on the meaning. For example, the hawk is the symbol of Horus the god of light, vision and speed. So when looking at the hawk these ancient Africans were not practicing animism, but simply using an image that would draw the followers immediately to the qualities of Horus and not the god, Horus, himself.

It is for this very reason that God gave Moses the Ten Commandments that admonish us to, "not make unto [us] any graven image, or any likeness of anything that is in heaven above, or that is in the earth beneath, or that is in the water under the earth" (Exodus 20:4).

Imam Warith Deen Muhammad, quoted in Akbar's *Chains and Images of Psychological Slavery,* speaks to the impact of images or inadequate social development that it engenders. He raises concern that is focused on Caucasians:

> What would happen to the minds of Caucasian people if Black people would suddenly come into power with their mentality, with their love for their religion? What would happen if nappy-headed, Black Jesuses were put all over their land and through out their homes, and in all of their churches? What would happen to their minds over a period of three hundred years if they kept coming to churches and seeing our image as their redeemer, seeing our image as their prophets, their apostles, their angels? They would be reduced to inferiority because the image before them of the supreme model of superiority would be "Black" and not "White."

Dr. (Na'im) Akbar further comments in the same book on the impact of the image of Jesus with this psychoanalysis:

> The influence of this Caucasian image on the psyches of non-Caucasian people is no worse than would be the influence of a Black image on the psyches of non-Black people. The reduction of people to a state of inferiority represents a reprehensible form of mind control of the worst kind. It also becomes the basis for insuring the continued psychological enslavement of any people under such an influence! (exclamation by author).

You see the mind functions syllogistically or in logic circuits. If you are presented with the false image of Jesus as a White man and then told that image is the Son of God; you have the perfect formula for the progression to a mentally ill state of mind – and a people totally economically, mentally and spiritually enslaved.

Elementary logic tells us that when the major premise that we are given is accepted as true, when it is really false, then every conclusion made thereafter will be incorrect.

When told that the Michelangelo painting of Jesus is the *Son of God*, the mind then concludes that Jesus' Father, God, is White. If God is good, then the White man is seen as good. If God is great, then the White man is great, while concomitantly the Black man is bad and inferior. The net effect is for Blacks to hate themselves and worship Whites.

Inspite of God's commandment to Moses that thou should have no graven image, we must remind ourselves that, as Christians, Jesus is the number one authority that we should look to in determining what we should do. There is a Christian book currently on the market by Charles and Garrett Sheldon titled *What Would Jesus Do?* which is marketed with a plethora of "WWJD" paraphernalia. But we should not limit ourselves to what would Jesus do, but rather with the clear facts where possible, by what *did* Jesus do? And when we look at the Gospels we see that Jesus did not allow Deuteronomic laws to prohibit Him from freeing spiritually and mentally enslaved souls. He healed on the Sabbath! He allowed His disciples to pick corn on the Sabbath! (Matthew 12:1-13) He ministered to undesirables whom the external religionists of His day shunned and avoided! As such, I think that Jesus would obviously approve of the Black (true) image of Jesus portrayed at Union Temple Baptist Church. Why? Because the way we feel about ourselves and about White people will not change by it self. Since we have a mental problem it must be dealt with psychologically. There are three steps then, that must be taken:

1. The first step must be ***psychotherapy or insight therapy*** – that is insight into the nature of the problem. We have already related the deep and profound psychological effect that the image of a White Christ has had on the psyche of Black people.
2. The second step must be ***aversion therapy.*** A catalyst must be induced to change the way we feel towards our selves and towards White people.
3. The third step must be ***behavior modification*** where we begin to act and feel a new way because of the different image of God. We will not stop criticizing and hating Black people and referring to our own as "they" and "them" while referring to Whites in glowing terms until such a psychological "de-brainwashing" occurs.

We need to understand that the subconscious does not argue about whether the thoughts we give it are good or bad, true or false, but it responds according to our suggestion. When the conscious, knowing or rational mind, is held in abeyance (checked or bypassed) and we entertain images and emotions while in a trance, we can arouse the cosmic forces of power within us. For example, ordinarily a person when conscious cannot be convinced that he is a dog and be made to get on all fours and begin barking. However, under hypnosis, the conscious mind can be put to sleep and this same suggestion can be made directly to the subconscious mind. Such a person under hypnosis will begin to bark and hop around on all fours like a dog.

In the case of the man whose son was being crushed by the old Cadillac, the same principle was at work. At a point of intensely heightened emotion at the sight of his son being crushed, his state of mind was altered so that in an almost trance-like state he suggested to himself (auto suggestion) that he *must* move the car off of his son.

Similarly in this age of chronic substance abuse, most of us have seen persons under the influence of drugs exercise inordinate and sometimes almost supernatural power. It is not the drugs, but under the influence of drugs such persons begin to say things like – "I am God." "I am superman," though they may be a "90 pound weakling." It then takes several hospital attendants and policemen to hold them down because they are now tapped into power they would not ordinarily be able to be manifest. The subconscious is under orders and it carries out its instructions.

Dr. Khalid Al-Mansour in his book, *The Pentecostals, the Good, the Bad and the Ugly,* states that: "It may well be that the code to divine healing rests with the effective ability of (church) saints to induce the subject to visualize himself as healed and believe that it will occur soon, and already begin to enjoy and thank God for the blessing."

He further states that a similar phenomenon occurs in martial arts. A karate student is trained to break a concrete block with his bare hand by being taught to visualize his hand not above, or even making contact with the surface of the block, but always beneath the block, with the block crumbling to the ground.

In recent years, a new theory of biological message transmission has evolved. It maintains that there are energy impulses that travel throughout the body. These body systems, we are told, consist of billions of nerves, neurons, and synapses. The view maintains that the electrical impulses comprising the message units duplicate themselves at the synapses until the message reaches its destination. This data, at the synapses some scientists believe, is capable of being manipulated under certain circumstances to trick the body into performing abnormal tasks. For instance, by properly imagining yourself healed of cancer, you trick the immune system into instantaneously manufacturing antibodies to effectuate the cure. If you do not maintain that "trick," you can experience a reversal. Perhaps this is why Jesus enjoined newly healed believers to "see that no man know it" (Matthew 8:4) because they might be subjected to the skeptical and derogatory criticisms of the unbelieving. This might tend to undo the benefits they had received at the hands of Jesus if others deposited thoughts of fear, doubt and anxiety in the subconscious mind.

In a documented case at Washington Hospital Center in the nation's capitol in recent years, two patients' folders were inadvertently switched. One person was diagnosed as having cancer, but was given the folder of a woman who did not have cancer. Meanwhile, the woman who did not have cancer was given the folder of the woman who did have cancer. Because each believed what was wrongfully in her folder, the one who didn't have cancer died, and the woman who did have cancer was still living at last report. Both responded to the results based on believing what was in their folders.

Needless to say, many of us today are in situations, circumstances, and predicaments because we have believed the false information placed in our folders. Based on this knowledge I believe that AIDS (Acquired Immune Deficiency Sydrome) can be healed. To cure AIDS the key would be to:

1. Induce the subject to believe that he/she will be healed through the power of God. (Prayers, shouting and dancing and testimonies along with the credibility of the minister and saints would reinforce belief in the subject).
2. The body's neurological/emotional system would then be tricked into believing the healing has occurred and therefore, create the necessary enzymes for healing, (by rejoicing and accepting the healing, the immune system would conform to produce the needed chemicals for the healing).
3. The individual would be insulated from doubters and naysayers, lest there be a reversal.

It thusly appears that once the subconscious receives a message with enough frequency, that message will become a habit that we accept as part of us. Stop to think about your habits. How many do you have that are not good for your mental, physical, and spiritual health? Smoking, drinking, drugging, overeating, nail-biting, feeling depressed or cynical–these are all subconscious habits that are learned. They suggest a self-esteem problem that must be changed to bring about permanent change. The other possibility of immediate change is for someone to tell us, "If you don't stop doing it, you are going to die."

The fact remains that we can change. We need to learn enough about how our mind functions so we can get it to work *for* us, rather than *against* us. One mechanism we should understand is the Reticular Activating System, a small network of cells, about the size of a crabapple at the base of the brain. It is your own built-in "apple computer." It has the unique function of filtering incoming sensory stimuli (sight, sound, smell and touch) and determining which ones are going to make an impression on the mind. It decides what information from moment to moment, will become a part of your world. Do you know any people who say they want your help, but continue to fail? Have you seen or heard of individuals who always seem to be looking for trouble? What they don't realize is that they have tuned their Reticular Activating System to guard their minds against success by deliberately seeking the negative inputs and problems they are trying to avoid.

This "R.A.S" can program you to be on the alert for success-related inputs. It will wake you up in the morning without an alarm clock. For years I have awakened exactly to the minute at the time I want to arise without the use of an alarm clock.

When my two sons were younger I had to awaken them every morning except Saturday. I had to get them up Monday through Friday to go to school and on Sunday to go to church. But because on Saturday something very important to them called "cartoons" was coming on television, they programmed their RAS to wake them up early every Saturday morning.

When the former mayor of Washington, DC was arrested in the now infamous crack-smoking incident, I began to minister to him. After his release from prison we were invited to appear on *Good Morning America,* a national morning television show. The night previous I told him to repeat over and over for forty-five minutes that in our appearance the next morning:

1. No question would be asked by the host of the show that we would not be able to answer.
2. We would be in total control of the interview.
3. We would be in total agreement about everything we said.

Well, the interview was scheduled to be an eight minute segment, but once we started the host became so engrossed in the interview that he said – "I don't know what's happening here, but we are going to skip our break and continue this interview." We were in complete accord on everything that we said and no question was asked that we were not ready for.

After the show, we went to breakfast. Former Mayor Marion Barry said that he believed in what I had told him and he had added that he would not perspire because it made observers think that he had still been using drugs. He said – "Did you notice that I did not perspire"?

He went on to say that he trusted and believed what I had told him to do because of a visit from a prison psychologist. The former mayor said that in his leisure time he played ping-pong everyday with an opponent who had a vicious backhand that he could never return. That caused him to lose many games. The psychologist told him to close his eyes and visualize the opponent's backhand shot until he could see it and then to see himself being able to return it. He said that the next day he was able to beat this opponent repeatedly.

This RAS system explains trouble-prone people as well as success-prone people. It clearly shows us how careful we must be in what we give importance to in our thinking.

The mind can control our bodies and our thoughts and can give us a natural high or make us ill. As we mentioned earlier, the subconscious mind controls all functions of the body. Whether awake or sound asleep, the subconscious mind controls all the vital functions of your body without the help of our conscious mind. For example while you are asleep your heart continues to beat, your lungs don't rest, and your breathing continues.

Physically, when we were created in the womb of our mother, our brain was the first thing created and everything else grew and sprouted from the brain in the same pattern that a plant grows. All of our physical body sprouted from the seed of our brain and the stem of our spinal column. But the brain is not just the root and seed of our physical existence; it is also the root of our mental and spiritual existence. The brain (mind) is the root of everything. Everything in the physical world was formed from an idea. So since the mind created the body, it is easy to see how the mind can heal the body. Any creator of a thing can repair or remake what it created.

The Addiction Research Foundation at Stanford University found in 1971 that our brains contained natural hormones including endorphin, and dynophin – all natural pain relievers many times more powerful than morphine. We manufacture these morphine-like substances in our own bodies to block pain and give us a natural high.

In a test using endorphin, researchers injected minute amounts of this hormone into men and women suffering from cancer. From a single injection, they all felt relief from their pain for one to three days.

Dennis Waitley reports in his book, *Seeds of Greatness,* that in 1978 at the University of California there was another discovery relating to the "placebo effect" which literally means, "I shall please." Placebos are inert substances (sometimes sugar) given to people along with experimental drugs. The drug's effect is tested by measuring the difference in responses to the powerless placebo and the drug. In a test where volunteers had their teeth extracted the subjects received a placebo, which they believed to be morphine. The placebo recipients reported that they experienced dramatic pain relief. However, when a drug that blocked the effects of the endorphin was given to them the pain returned almost immediately. The test confirmed something important to understand. When a placebo is given, and the individual believes he or she is getting relief, the brain releases chemicals to substantiate the belief. In many respects the placebo effect is an act of faith. If our thoughts can produce natural endorphins that are 50-190 times as powerful as morphine, is it not possible for us to use this same power of faith in our everyday lives, with the only side effect being happiness and the power to rise above any situation, circumstance or obstacle? This is how the mind works!

The Genius of Jesus Revealed

Chapter VIII

In the preface to his book, *Jesus and the Disinherited,* Howard Thurman begins by stating that "the significance of the religion of Jesus to people with their backs against the wall [is always] crucial". He goes on to raise the question: "Why does Christianity seem impotent to deal radically with the manifold problems of inequity and injustice facing the masses of oppressed people in the world?" It is from this launching pad that he makes a serious divergence from what Vincent Harding calls the "strange mutation [called] American (Eurocentric) Christianity" and reveals the betrayal of the genius of Jesus.

We have already referenced the "customized" version of Christianity presented to our ancestors by their slave masters during the time of slavery. My friend, I. Barashango, in his work, *God, the Bible and the Black Man's Destiny,* not only substantiates the African origin of Christianity in terms of personalities and concepts; but at the same time documents distortions in concepts that define the European takeover of the African Church and religion. In chapters titled, "How Did Black Christianity become White Christianity?" and "The Rise of the Counterfeit Church;" he offers the following insight: "The Roman Church... produced very little [foundational or fundamental ideas] of itself. It merely co-opted the genius of the African Church (the mother church) and perverted it with European [culture concepts]."

Most of us who are Christians have absolutely no knowledge about how we came to be Christians. As mentioned earlier, the majority of us call ourselves "Christians" because our parents call themselves "Christians." And they called themselves Christians, and their parents called themselves "Christians" because their parents called themselves "Christians." But why? Was it because Jesus, Himself, came down from the celestial sphere to the slave plantation one day and declared us to be Christian? No, Jesus did not!! So, who was it that gave our foreparents our teachings about Christianity? It was our slave masters who gave us their own "customized" version of Christianity. And our foreparents for the most part accepted the White man's version of Christianity with no questions asked. So it is absolutely certain that we did not receive the "true" word of God or the "true" message of Jesus. We accepted our Christianity from the same slave masters who made us slave for them;

the same slave owners who broke up our families, raped our mothers and sisters, beat, dismembered, castrated, hung, and lynched us!!

Think about this! Why would an oppressor who has spent the majority of his time, abusing, misusing, and trying to kill and destroy us, and our minds, turn around and give us a message that would empower and enlighten us?

Christianity as we have been taught it, then, is only the White slave masters teachings about God, Jesus, and Christianity. We have never been really taught the true teachings of Jesus. What we have been taught is the teachings of the White slave master with Jesus' name on it.

As you may know, for a long period of time during slavery, we were not allowed to even touch the Bible or to read it for ourselves. If caught doing so our hands would be cut off. In Africa, my Ghanaian brothers and sisters tell me that they were told that they would go blind if they dared to try to read the Bible on their own.

And now that we can read the Bible, after several hundred years of brainwashing and programming – the slave master's teachings have made us so oblivious to the truth of Jesus' message that we continue today to have little or no knowledge about the true religion of Jesus.

There is a great irony to be amplified here. Though as Barashango points out, the African Church is the mother church of Christianity, the Black Church, as we know it, grew out of the White Christian church of America. Bishop William J. Walls points out that "...we see that all the Black churches were born in White congregations East and West, North and South." He goes on to state that the "White church establishment is, in fact, the "mother" of the Black Church.

"All of what the Black Church knows is from Westernized Christianity, when in the beginning, Africans created the first religions." Bishop Walls continues:

> ...the Christian religion came to America by way of Europe, although it was born in Asia and grew up in Africa and Southern Europe. The Black Church has never defined its religion for itself. It established itself after the same Western religion that excluded the African origin and presence in Christianity. And as much as it professes how much it loves the Bible and the teachings of the Bible, the Black church has never deeply studied the origins and interpretations of the Bible for itself.

Any basic historical analysis of European Christianity reveals that it was this same institution that initiated and established the slave trade. It was the Catholic Pope in 1411, who declared Africans to be "soulless individuals".

During the time of slavery in America, religion was used to continue the mental enslavement of Africans in America.

According to Walls, "Negro enrollment in Christian churches really ballooned in the 18th century." During this period African Christians in America decided to establish their own churches because they could not worship, freely and unencumbered in the White church. This is why in 1794 Richard Allen founded the A.M.E. Church and Absalom Jones founded the African Protestant Episcopal Church. They did not separate from the White churches because of the dogma and doctrine that sanctioned oppression and racial atrocities against people of African heritage. They separated and formed themselves after the same system that helped enslave them. According to E. Franklin Frazier in his book, *The Negro Church in America*, Richard Allen and Absalom Jones "differed as to whether Negroes should model their church organization after the Methodist or after the Protestant Episcopal Church." The point to remember is that the Eurocentric interpretation of Christianity would be the model without any modification.

This is a brief history of how the religion of Christianity was "given" to Africans in America. And to this day this religion is designed to hurt us far more than help us. History accurately records that White America has never given African Americans anything that has helped the masses of our people in this country. We can climb the ladder of success, but we must do it one at a time and bring nobody else along with us.

And we must come to realize and accept the chilling and penetrating truth that as we go into a new millennium, African Americans still do not operate out of an African theology.

To have an authentic African or Black theology, its dogma or founding conceptualization must be from the African way or Africentric. Incorporating or using African surface structure forms, — i.e. wearing Kente cloth robes, using African drums, icons and decorations does not make a church Africentric. That is just "Blackenizing" White theology. Even the so-called Black Liberation Theology movement, for the most part, is simply White theology with Black faces decorated with a little Kente cloth. Black liberation theology has essentially interpreted theology within the established White framework. The foundational dogma and doctrine as interpreted by the White slave master has remained intact. It was designed for pacification and to support the authority of rich and powerful White supremacy. It was the kind of religion that met the needs of the Whites and not the needs of the oppressed. C. Eric Lincoln touches on the basic concept that the response of a church or a religion to social change is distinguished as either "internal" or "external" alertness. "Internal alertness" pertains to foundational matters of church or religious dogma. "External alertness," on the other hand, pertains to functional matters of church or religious practice. I submit that the African American church religion has since slavery remained unaffected and essentially unchanged fundamentally. According to Dr. Ben-Jochanan, we can still observe in the African American community a proliferation of our Black seminarians and Black clergy without a Black theology. Our "internal alertness" has not changed!!! Years ago Bishop Henry Neal Turner said:

> ...the White man's digest of Christianity or Bible doctrines are not suited to the wants, manhood, growth, and progress of the Negro. Indeed he has colored the Bible in his translation to suit the White man, and made it, in many respects, objectionable to the Negro. And until a company of learned Black men shall rise up and re-translate the Bible, it will not be wholly acceptable and in keeping with the higher conceptions of the Black man. We need a new translation of the Bible for Colored churches.

Bishop Alexander McGuire, chaplain of the UNIA under Marcus Garvey, sought to replace all vestiges of Anglo-Saxonized versions of Christianity with an Africanized version way back in the 1920s.

Howard Thurman states that, "there is one overmastering problem that the socially and politically disinherited always face: under what terms is survival possible?" In the case of the [African Hebrews] in the Greco Roman world he says that [this] "problem was even more acute than under ordinary circumstances, because it had to do not only with physical survival in terms of life and limb, but also the actual survival of a culture and a faith". Thurman's account here is most instructive because this is the same exact dilemma facing African Americans today and other oppressed people today.

It is in such a "psychological climate that Jesus began his teaching and his ministry. His message was directed to the oppressed masses in Rome." That message says Thurman, "focused on the urgency of a radical change in the inner attitude of the people. He recognized fully that 'out of the heart flows the issues of life,' and that no external force, however great and overwhelming, can at long last destroy a people if it does not first win the victory of the spirit against them."

The urgent question was: What must be the attitude toward Rome? Thurman states that "this is the position of the disinherited in every age. What must be the attitude toward the rulers, the controllers of political, social, and economic life?" Thurman proposes that "two alternatives opened to the [African Hebrew] minority of which Jesus was apart – resistance or non-resistance."

Under non-resistance one position can be that of an imitator i.e. assimilate into the culture of the dominant group. In the common language of today a person taking such a position would be deemed an "Uncle Tom sellout." Thurman points out that the "upper class" Sadducees were an example of this attitude. "They seemed to love Rome more than they loved their own people. They saw as their only option to either 'become like the Romans or be destroyed by the Romans.' They chose the former."

The other alternative in the non-resistance position is to offer no resistance to the oppressor while simply carrying silent and unspoken contempt for him. The opposite alternative to non-resistance is, of course, resistance. This resistance can be in the first instance a mental attitude. It can also take the form of armed revolt. Thurman states:

> With only these two alternatives Jesus came up with yet another. Jesus expressed his alternative in a brief formula –
> The Kingdom of God is within us. The solution which Jesus found for Himself and His people as they faced the wicked hostility of the Roman world "becomes the world and work of redemption for all cast down people in every generation and in every age."

Jesus taught what was first taught in the ancient mystery systems of Kemet (Black Egypt) – "entering the Kingdom of God," awakening the hidden power of God that resides in man. His response as taught to his fellow oppressed brothers and sisters in a racist White power structure in Rome, was to adopt a system of practices aimed at awakening the dormant higher faculties. This was Jesus' primary focus – entering the Kingdom of God.

This simple and yet so powerful recognition is what made ancient Egypt the greatest, most advanced and powerful civilization to ever grace the planet. Ra Un Neter Amen, writing in his book, *Metu Neter, Volume II – The Kamitic Initiation System,* states that:

> It is unfortunate that the millions of people who have witnessed

> the great accomplishments in art, mathematics, architecture, etc. of ancient Egypt, have not understood that the singular cause for such accomplishments was the people's devotion to a way of life in which the priests exhorted the population to identify with the divine aspect of their being as their true selves and to strive to realize the ideals symbolizing it [their divinity] in their daily lives. It is the only way that a nation can survive for the close to four thousand years that enabled Kamit (ancient Egypt) to accumulate the knowledge, and continuity of works that have come down to us as its great legacy of accomplishment. This higher part of man's being with which we must identify, the divine in man's being, the Ancient Egyptians symbolized as *Ausar*. Around this symbol was developed an entire way of life, and system of spiritual development which became the world's oldest documented and longest lived religion in the world (it lasted over four thousand years) – the Ausarian Religion. The fundamental principle governing the Ausarian Religion is the reality... that man is made in the likeness of God. By this it is meant that God's traits reside in man as his/her essential qualities. "Anuk Ausar," "I am Ausar" (I am divine); these were the words, backed with substance that [if oppressed people could understand, articulate and manifest today would be able to totally free themselves of the mental, economic, social and religious shackles that continue to keep them bound].

This is exactly Jesus' answer to the oppressed people with their backs against the wall – "the Kingdom of God is within." Thurman says this is "the core of the analysis of Jesus...man is a Child of God, the God of life!" This is a life-giving, life-saving transformation to the "socially disadvantaged man" who "is constantly given a negative answer to the most important personal questions upon which mental health depends: 'Who am I?' 'What am I?'" (Thurman).

The lot, state and position of the masses of people professing Jesus Christ as their Savior would be changed overnight if this idea first put forth in ancient Kemet (Egypt) and ultimately by Jesus was understood and grasped.

It is no doubt in my mind why Jesus selected Peter as his first disciple and ultimately said that "upon this rock" (upon Peter's spiritual understanding) he would establish his church. Peter stood out above all the other disciples. He had the irrepressible urge, the dogged determination to seek to understand issues. He was known for always asking "Why?" It was through Peter's persistence in asking questions that initiated an exchange that developed a special relationship between Jesus and Peter.

You see, Peter, like so many who feel inferior and are oppressed today, had a very low self-esteem and self-concept when he initially met Jesus. Someone in his family, perhaps his mother or father had named him Simon – which literally means "shaky, flaky like a leaf." Perhaps this was the beginning of the use of the phrase "Simple Simon." Regardless, Peter internalized this name and grew to be a very impulsive and by some estimations a very unbalanced, unpredictable individual. But just as many oppressed people today have been labeled and thereby dogged by a sense of personal and social inferiority, or both, when Peter met Jesus he became, as Howard Thurman says, "*immunized* against the most radical threats against self-worth and self-value." Jesus simply changed his name from "shaky flaky" (Simon) to "Solid as a Rock" (Peter). What did Jesus really do when he changed Peter's name? He lifted Peter to the status of a "Child of God" and "stabilized his ego." Thurman warns that:

> this alone is not enough, but without it nothing else is of value. And once the question of "Who am I?" has been answered, one of the practical results is the ability to make an objective, detached appraisal of other people, particularly one's antagonists. [Then] after sure grounding of [your] sense of personal worth and dignity, [you are] in a position to appraise [your] own intrinsic powers, gifts, talents and abilities. [Such a redeemed individual] no longer views his equipment through the darkened lenses of those who are largely responsible for his social predicaments. He can think of himself with some measure of detachment from the shackles of his immediate world: The psychological effect on the individual of the conviction that he is a child of God gives a note of integrity to whatever he does. It provides character in the sense of sure knowledge and effective performance.

Peter's faith in the Spiritual Man, Jesus, quickened Peter's spiritual understanding. Peter's faith opened up his spiritual discernment so that when Jesus asked him "Who do men say that the Son of Man is? the disciples, looking upon the personality as the real thing, said: "Some say 'John the Baptist,' some, 'Elijah,' and others, 'Jeremiah,' or one of the prophets." But Jesus asked: "But who say ye that I am?" Only Peter answered, "Thou art the Christ, the Son of the Living God." And Jesus then answered, [and] "Thou art Peter, and upon this rock I will build my Church, and the gates of Hell shall not prevail against it. I will give unto thee the keys of the Kingdom of heaven" (Matthew 16:13-19).

Peter recognized God incarnate in Jesus. He recognized the indwelling of God in Jesus. It is to this faith in the understanding of the real being of Man that Jesus gave power in earth and heaven. It was not to the personal Peter that Jesus gave the keys to the Kingdom, but to all of us who are conscious (aware) of the indwelling power of God in Man (us). This is the "key" to success, power and dominion over the earth.

It is very important to point out now that all of the religious movements that have affected the masses of our oppressed community and led to economic, social, and spiritual advancement of a great number of people have all taught the "God incarnate in man concept." Hans A. Baer in his classic study, *The Black Spiritual Movement: A Religious Response to Racism,* contends that "the grassroots religious organizations all protested against the racist and social stratification of American society." They all, as did Jesus, sought to make the harsh life of oppressed people tolerable as well as insure their own survival. Farad Muhammad, Bishop George Hurley, Noble Drew Ali, Marcus Garvey, Elijah Muhammad, Daddy Grace, Father Divine and others of lesser repute all taught what Jesus taught – that God is not up in the sky somewhere, in the church, temple or synagogue, but in Man. As well, states Adib Rashad (James Miller) in his book, *Elijah Muhammad and the Ideological Foundation of the Nation of Islam*, "while there are specific differences among the doctrines they espoused, their respective preachments contained profound life–saving similarities:"

1. They taught that Blacks have a glorious past.
2. The Black man is the original man.
3. The Black man was god.
4. Blacks should renounce Christianity or at least the White man's version of Christianity.
5. Blacks would again rise to their rightful place in the world.
6. Each preacher of salvation proclaimed himself to be a messenger, prophet, and a god.

But above all each taught ***God incarnate in Man***!! They each practiced the reality that Jesus is the expression of the highest possibility of Man; of what God in the form of Man should be.

1. Bishop George Hurley taught his congregations that the ***Spirit of God is "imbedded in each man*** and said that a new form of Chris-

tianity must beushered into existence or a recapturing of the lost form of African Christianity."

2. Elijah Muhammad often pronounced that "***whenever you see a Black man, you are looking at God***."
3. Noble Drew Ali taught his followers of the two-selves; the higher divine self and the lower self. ***The higher self was the human spirit clothed with soul, made in the form of Allah (God).***
4. Father Divine started out teaching his congregation that "***God resides in everyone and therefore everyone is in essence God or part of God.***" He later changed from this concept of God to the idea that God is in Father Divine only.
5. Bishop Charles Mason, founder of the Church of God In Christ taught "by sanctification we are saved from the power and root of sin and restored to the ***IMAGE OF GOD.***" We "grow up in all things into Him that is our head; till we attain the measure of the stature of the fullness of Christ." His church cohort Charles Price Jones reflects Mason's theology of God incarnate in man in the motto he coined around 1900 – "Christ all in all; no more I, but Christ."
6. Marcus Garvey – Garvey preached that the ***Black man was a God*** and "Africanized Christianity [as] Muhammad Africanized Islam."
7. Daddy Grace, Marcelino Manuel De Graca, came to America from the Cape Verde Islands. He was of mixed ancestry (African and Portugese) and had some knowledge of African theological systems. He told his followers he was the "grace of the world" and that ***God thusly was incarnate in him.***

Before we explore in a deeper fashion the impact and value of the permeation of these "religio nationalist movements" with the "***God incarnate in man concept***" let me validate the Africentricity and biblical and apostolic authenticity of their belief. First of all God incarnate in man is an Africentric concept. It is an African-based theological precept.

We have already referenced the evident identification of man with God in ancient Kemet (Egypt). It is also evident in indigenous African belief systems in other parts of Africa and throughout the Diaspora. Ra Un Neter Amen again notes that, "among the Bantu (a broad group of people occupying the southern portion of Africa, predominantly represented by the Zulus) the categorical name for both God and man is

Muntu.... God and man are grouped together because they both share in 'ubwenge,' which is the agency of the will acting upon the spirit."

Ulysses Duke Jenkins in his book, *Ancient African Religion and the African American Church,* says that awakening the hidden power of God that resides in man "is a spiritual quest that deals with touching the rhythmic energies of the cosmos, which is man's well of creative energy. This energy may be tapped by prayer, meditation or chanting. In the Yoruba traditional religion Ifa Divination system, the divine powers of God can be manifest in [priests called] Babalawos who go through secret training and preparation." Many Yoruba scholars such as Lucas and Oduyoye have traced the origin of the Yoruba back to ancient Egypt which would explain the secret initiation rites that are quite similar to the esoteric (secret) knowledge taught in the Mystery Temples in Egypt where some theorize Jesus studied.

What Robert Farris Thompson calls the "spiritualized militancy" of the "petro rite" (a ceremony that imbues the participant with a power and very presence of the God within) in Haiti forms the basis for the very negative portrait which causes great fear, disdain and hatred for the African rooted religion of Voodoo.

When the French attacked the Africans in Haiti, in an effort to subjugate them in the 1800s, they were soundly defeated by the Africans who, after ritualized services where they were "possessed" by the very essence of the spirit of God, were totally invincible and indomitable. Such was the power of believing that when they became "married to the spirit" the spirit of God, now dwelling *in* the practitioner of the religion could be shown or manifested *through* them in mighty acts of power. Naturally the imperialists of France and the rest of the Western world could not have a people believing that the very power of God was dwelling in them; so they labeled the religion "Voodoo" – as something evil, negative, heathenistic and satanic. "Evil and negative," mind you, because it resulted in the Africans, without any sophisticated weaponry or technology being able to defeat the much more well-tooled and modernly equipped army of the French.

For many, because of conditioning and programming, the idea that God can be in a man, and more alarmingly, in Black men, is a very horrifying and blasphemous thought. But this is exactly what Jesus taught. He told us to not worship Him, nor marvel at the things that He had done, because "greater works" than [His] were possible for those who followed Him and not worshipped Him (John 14:12). In fact, when one carefully reads John 10:32-35 it tells us the reason that the Jews sought to stone Jesus to death. Jesus asked them "for which of the many good works I shewed thee do ye stone me?" Their answer was, "for a good work we stone thee not, but for blasphemy; and because that thou, being a man, makest thyself God" (John 10:33). The idea that one raised in the ghetto of Nazareth would equate himself with God was absolutely unthinkable and inexcusable.

Dr. Na'im Akbar adds in an article titled *Allegorical Teachings of the Honorable Elijah Muhammad* that:

> the idea that God (Allah) had consistently intervened either personally or by a Messenger in the experiences of human beings from the very beginning of time, is a prominent reality in all peoples' religious stories and/or cultural myths.
>
> In ancient Kemet (called Egypt) divine personages frequently interacted in human circumstance. The same is true in Greek mythology, West African mythology, East Indian, Native Ameri can and the cultural myths of all people. This idea is repeatedly followed throughout the Holy Quran, the Torah, and the Bible. It would seem bizarre that God's (Allah's) commitment and demonstration of his intervention in the affairs of other people through out history would suddenly become an unimaginable occurrence in the affairs of a truly deserving people based upon their persistent faith, if nothing more!!

Well what are some tangible results evident in the previously named "religio nationalist" leaders and so few others who taught the "God incarnate in man concept?"

To begin with, though His message has been muted, muffled, and warped, Jesus remains one of the most influential powerful and widely revered figures in the history of the planet. His impact on individual lives has been monumental. The fact is, however, Jesus came with a message of corporate and not just individual salvation. Eurocentric Christianity helps the individual, if it helps anyone at all. White society has never given African Americans anything that has helped the majority of our people in this country. The message of "slave-taught Christianity" is then contrary to Jesus' teaching because he declares in Matthew 15:24 – "I am not sent but unto the lost sheep of the house of Israel" (corporate salvation). All of the religious leaders we will look closer at came with the same type of plan – a plan for the collective salvation of the masses of our oppressed community and they did it teaching the "God incarnate in Man concept" in varying ways and degrees. We will look at just a few of them:

Father Divine

According to Jill Watts in her book, *God, Harlem USA - The Father Divine Story* :

> Father Divine taught God incarnate in Man. George Baker as he was formerly called, amassed a financial fortune and helped countless thousands to rise from poverty. He taught that poverty resulted from negative thinking [and] he was one of the first ministers to reintroduce social relief and political activism to the Black church.
>
> He lived next door to former United States President Roosevelt in an elaborate estate in Hyde Park, New York. He said, "I am Divine," and that is not merely a word, it is power. He owned hotels, restaurants, gas stations, grocery stores, a clothing factory, a national newspaper, a bakery and an agricultural complex called "Hope Farm" which specialized in raising poultry. He owned farms in Kramville, Samsonville, Cherry Hill, Stone Ridge and New Paltz in New York, as well as numerous properties in California, Pennsylvania, Virginia, Maryland and a host of other states. He dared to confront the American government calling for "all nations and peoples who have suppressed and oppressed the underprivileged... be obliged to pay the African slaves and their descendants for all uncompensated servitude." (Reparations)

Napoleon Hill, world-famous author who studied great achievers and is the foremost scholar and thinker in the science of human success wrote this about Father Divine in his book, *You Can Work Your Own Miracles:*

> This man gave himself the very impressive pseudonym of "Father Divine." He gained a following estimated in the millions, including large numbers of Whites, located in nearly every state of the U.S. and in some foreign countries. Father Divine was given the stewardship of vast amounts of money. He traveled in a Rolls Royce and slept in his own hotels in many of the cities where he visited; so there was never a question of his staying in any but the pleasantest accommodations. The color bar

did not affect him. His huge complex organization operated many kinds of businesses, from pushcarts to dress shops and restaurants – all staffed by volunteer help. The secret of Father Divine's riches is not new to me. I have devoted over forty years to its study, and I have seen it work successfully in the lives of more than five hundred of the outstanding men of this nation. He was an uneducated Black man who changed his name from George Baker, [a cotton picking Negro,] to Father Divine. He believed that God dwelled in him and taught his followers for a time to believe the same about themselves. This was key to his great success.

Martin Luther King, Jr.

In his book, *Visions for Black Men*, Akbar says that [Dr. King] exemplified, better than anybody I have known in modern times, the quality of "courage." He faced the "beasts of Birmingham, the mad dogs of Selma, and the wild animals of Cicero." [As well] "he defied the mainstream of his own 'educated' class and stood up against his colleagues who were 'weak and passive and took the church to the street.'"

After reading in several books that Martin Luther King Jr. very often carried a copy of Thurman's *Jesus and the Disinherited* on his many civil rights journeys, I often pondered whether he had the message of "God incarnate in Man" etched on his heart. This I questioned until I spoke at a forum at Howard University's Rankin Chapel in the presence of Dr. King's cousin, Rev. R.T. Osburn, who is also a longstanding officer of the Southern Christian Leadership Conference (SCLC). When I finished my speech about the need for a theology that teaches what Jesus and Thurman espoused — "God incarnate in man," Rev. Osburn afterwards told me that Martin had spoken on that very subject in a speech at Selma, Alabama during the height of the civil rights struggle. Without the deep self-affirmation and power that comes with knowing that God is within you, I believe there is no way Dr. King could have exhibited the courage, strength, and leadership that he did. He was totally fearless because he knew that "greater [was the] (God) that was in him, than [the white-hot evil he faced in racist America] (I John 4:4).

Dr. Howard Thurman

Howard Thurman first published his book, *Jesus and the Disinherited,* in 1949. His interpretation of the Gospel of Jesus exposed Jesus' message as a living "instruction manual as to how the poor and disenfranchised can triumphantly survive [and be victorious]." The book helped shape Dr. Martin Luther King's philosophy and basically then was the textbook for the civil rights movement.

This "Black-prophet-mystic," as Vincent Harding called him, in a very scholarly and yet in a very reasonable and practical way showed the oppressed; "those who stand with their backs against the wall" – what he coined as the "religion of Jesus". This religion of Jesus, as aforementioned, taught the "the God incarnate in man concept" in direct opposition to the orthodox Christian teaching of the religion about Jesus.

In a very polite, and yet very straightforward way he (Thurman) challenged the racism in America that made "religion (Christianity) a defender and guarantor " [of Jim Crow and other racist mentalities]. He raised the question about the psychological impact on the disinherited of God,

> imaged as an elderly, benign White man, seated on a white throne, with bright, white light emanating from his countenance. Angels [who were] blondes and brunets suspended in the air around his throne, to be his messengers and execute his purposes; [While] Satan is viewed as being red with a glow of fire, [and] imps, the messengers of the devil, [as] black. The phrase 'black as an imp' is a stereotype.
>
> The implications of such a view are simply fantastic in the intensity of their tragedy, doomed on earth to a fixed and unremitting status of inferiority of which segregation is symbolic. And at the same time cut off from the hope that the Creator intended it otherwise, those who are thus victimized are stripped of all social protection.

This statement Thurman made in 1949, at a time when Black men were being lynched and castrated daily for doing and saying far less. Howard Thurman exhibited great boldness, courage and strength because he, too, knew that the Kingdom of God (Power of God) was dwelling within him. "To be assured of this (he says) becomes the answer to the threat of violence-yea, to violence itself. To the degree to which a man knows this, he is unconquerable from within and without."

He says in his book, *Jesus and the Disinherited,* that:

> When a man recognizes he is God's child [it] tends to shift the basis of his relationship with all his fellows. He recognizes at

once that to fear a man, whatever may be that man's power over him is a basic denial of the integrity of his very life.... Even the threat of violence, with the possibility of death that it carries, is recognized for what it is - merely the threat of violence with a death potential. Such a man recognizes that death cannot possibly be the worst thing in the world. There *are* some things that are worse than death. To deny one's own integrity of personality in the presence of human challenge is one of those things. "Be not afraid of them that kill the body, and after that have no more that they can do, says Jesus."

I cannot but believe that this truth from Thurman was resonating in the heart of Dr King as he spoke at Mason Temple in Memphis, Tennessee, the night before his assassination.

Elijah Muhammad

At the apex of what Elijah Muhammad taught exudes knowledge of what the Kingdom of God is, as it was originally taught in ancient Kemet. What the Greeks stole from Egypt and called the "Delphic Oracle" was the mandate that Muhammad made primary to being able to empower yourself. "Knowledge of self," he taught, is the key to power. This uneducated Black man, in teaching Black people, had in the words of Akbar "reached all the way back beneath the pyramids, down through the Temples of Karnak, looked through the documents of old and found the message written in the hieroglyphics, going back over 5,000 years that said, "Man, know thyself." Akbar continues:

> This little Black man, one of the giants among men the world over, was the one who provided the... system that turned Malcolm X from a hustler, pimp, and drug dealer to the great, eloquent, powerful leader that he became. No other organization, church, temple or mosque, (Akbar continues), took nobodies and made them somebodies. Dr. King talked about being somebody. Elijah Muhammad showed you how to make nobodies into somebodies. He restored chronic junkies, longstanding prostitutes, longstanding recidivistic criminals, the downtrodden, the down-and-outs who the psychologists, criminologists, sociologists, social workers, preachers, teachers, and nobody else could do anything with. He led masses of such people in owning a bank, a trucking company, schools, all over the nation, and thousands of acres of land.

How did he do it?

He taught the Black man to know self and in knowing self, Black men discovered the Power of God within. They discovered their true nature as the offspring (the sons and daughters of God — Little Gods!! And, God can do anything!!

Elijah Muhammad often said, "when you see the Black man, you are looking at God."

Marcus Garvey

Marcus Garvey came to the United States between 1917 and 1920 from Jamaica to start a chapter of his Jamaican organization, the Universal Negro Improvement Association. By Dr. Al Mansour's account, "In a short three years he was proclaimed the only mass leader the race has ever had, before or since. In that short time his following rose from 100 people to four to six million at a time when the entire African American population was somewhere between nine to ten million." In the same span of three years he packed Madison Square Garden in New York and raised $10 million from the poor Black masses without assistance from the White media, Black middle class, or White power structure. Dr. Khalid Al-Mansour says that amount would be equivalent to raising about $20 million today. As well, Garvey infused in former slaves a positive strength based on pride in African heritage.

He practiced the African theological concept of Henotheism – the acceptance of other religions. He had Muslim, Christian, and traditional African religions in his organization. There were Muslims who agitated for Islam to be declared the official religion of the UNIA, while Christian clergy wanted Christianity to be the anchor of the organization. He remained receptive to them all without declaring either to be the favored. Because of this Africentric belief, he was able to bring together more Africans on the continent and throughout the Diaspora than any man before or since.

Garvey led the organization in owning an internationally distributed newspaper, a shipping line called the Black Star, and a plethora of other businesses. He brought together more Africans in America, the continent of Africa, the Caribbean, South America and the entire Western world than any man in the history of the planet.

And once again at the root of his great success in all of his endeavors was the belief that the "Anglo-Saxonized" version of Christianity had to be replaced with an "Africanized version." He exhorted UNIA followers to reject the European concept of God and Jesus and to see God as a Black man, and themselves thusly as beings in the image of God. Garvey, too, taught his followers to know self and love self – not in terms of personality or even cultural identity but, in a deeper sense, as beings in the image and likeness of God, with almost unlimited potential.

Given the monumental achievements of just a few of the great Black men who taught that God resides in man, one can readily see the power and strength in such a concept. Howard Thurman says that "once the ego is stabilized [by] the awareness of being a Child of God (in His image and likeness), [it] results in a new courage, fearlessness and power." You saw it happening again and again in the lives of the men just discussed.

All of the aforementioned persons truly understood what it means to be a Child of God. So Thurman is clear when he says:

> To the Child of God, a scale of values becomes available by which men are measured and their true significance determined. Even the threat of violence, with the possibility of death that it carries, is recognized for what it is – merely the threat of violence with a death potential. Such a man recognizes that death cannot possibly be the worst thing in the world.
>
> One of the practical results following such an orientation is the ability to make an objective, detached appraisal of other people, particularly one's antagonists. If a person is grounded in a sense of personal worth and dignity, then he is in a position to appraise his own intrinsic powers, gifts, talents and abilities.

Such a person's achievements and accomplishments are then both unlimited and immeasurable.

All things are possible through the tremendous insight of Jesus–the Genius of Jesus Revealed!!

Bibliography

1. *Abhedananda, Swami,* ***Kashmiri O. Tibbetti***, Bengali, Calcutta.
2. *Akbar, Na'im,* ***The Community of Self***, Tallahassee, Florida, Mind Productions 1985, Revised printing 1991.
   Chains and Images of Psychological Slavery, Jersey City, New Jersey 1984.
   Visions for Black Men, Nashville, Tennessee, Winston Derek Publishing Inc., 1991.
3. *Al-Mansour, Abdullah Tariq, Dr.,* ***The Lost Books of Africa Rediscovered***, San Francisco, California, The First Arabian Press 1991.
   The Pentecostals, The Good, The Bad and The Ugly San Francisco, California, The First African Press, 1991.
4. *Ani, Marimba* ***Yurugu, An African Centered Critique of European Cultural Thought and Behavior,*** *Trenton, New Jersey, Africa World Press Inc., 1994.*
5. *Amen, Ra Un Neter* ***Metu Neter Vol. 2-Anuk-Ausar- The Kamitic Initiation System,*** Brooklyn, New York, Khamit Corp., 1994.
6. Ashby, Muata, ***Egyptian Yoga, The Philosophy of Enlightenment,*** Cruzian Mystic Books, Miami Florida, 1995.
7. Baer, Hans A., ***The Black Spiritual Movement: A Religious Response to Racism***, Knoxville, Tennessee, The University of Tennessee Press, 1984.
8. Barashango, I., ***God, the Bible and the Black Man's Destiny*** Washington, DC., IV Dynasty, 1982.
9. Ben-Jochanan, ***Our Black Seminarians and Black Clergy Without a Black Theology***, New York, Alkebulan Books, 1978.
10. Bernal, Martin, ***Black Athena: The Afro-Asiatic Roots of Classical Civilization***, New Brunswick, New Jersey, Rutgers University Press, 1987.
11. Blyden, Edward W., ***Christianity, Islam and the Negro Race,*** Baltimore, Maryland, Black Classic Press, 1988, Reprint 1994.
12. Bock, Janet., ***The Jesus Mystery: Of Lost Years and Unknown Travels***, Los Angeles, California, Aura Books- Division Aura Enterprise, 1980.
13. Browder, Tony., ***From the Browder File***, Washington, DC,

The Institute of Karmic Guidance, 1989.
Nile Valley Contributions to Civilization, Washington, DC, The Institute of Karmic Guidance, 1992.

14. Bunyan, John., ***Pilgrim's Progress,*** United States by Dodd, Mead & Company Inc., 1979, 1st published in England in 1678.
15. Bultman, Rudolph, ***The Second Letter to the Corinthians***, Minneapolis, Minnesota, Augsburg, 1985.
The Significance of the Historical Jesus for the Theology of Paul in Faith and Understanding, Collected Essays, London, England SCM, 1969.
16. Carter, Lawerence, E., ***Nile Valley Civilization*** (quote taken from the book ***What They Never Told You in the Class,*** New York Luxor Publications, 1983 by Indus Khamit Kush
17. Casey, M., ***From Jewish Prophet to Gentile God***, Cambridge, England, Clark, 1991.
18. Charroux, Robert, ***The Mysterious Unknown***, London, England, Neville Spearman Ltd., 1972.
19. Cleage Jr., Rev. Albert B., ***Black Christian Nationalism: New Directions for the Black Church***, New York Quill Paperbacks (Morrow) 1972, Second Printing Luxor Publishers of the Pan Africans Orthodox Christian Church, Detroit, Michigan, 1987.
20. Chopra, Deepak, E., ***The Seven Spiritual Laws of Success***, San Rafael, California, Amber Allen Publishing and New World Library, 1993.
21. Clemmons, Bishop Ithiel C., ***Bishop C.H. Mason and the Roots of the Church of God In Christ,*** Bakersfield, California, Pneuma Life Publishing Company, 1996.
22. Covey, Stephen R., ***The Seven Habits of Highly Effective People,*** New York, Fireside Books (Simon & Schuster), 1989.
23. Doresse, Jean, ***The Secrets Books of the Egyptian Gnostics***, Rochester, Vermont Inner Traditions International, 1986.
24. Dowling, Levi H., ***The Aquarian Gospel of Jesus Christ*** Marina del Rey, California, 1907; Fourteenth Printing Devorss and Company, 1993.
25. Durant, Will, ***Caesar and Christ***, New York, 1944.
26. East, Charles Henry, ***An Unscientific Scientist [?] In a Scientist World,*** The Golden Age Magazine of the Jehovah's Witness denomination. July 15, 1925.

27. El-Amin, Mustafa, ***Free Masonry, Ancient Egypt and the Islamic Destiny***, Jersey City, New Jersey, New Mind Productions, 1988.
28. Evans, Tony Dr., ***What Matters Most***, Chicago, Illinois, Moody Press, 1997.
29. Ferrell, John, ***Fruit of Creations - A Look at Global Substainability as Seen Through the Eyes of George Washington Carver***, Wynnewood, Pennsylvania, Macalester Park Printing Company, 1995.
30. Frazier, Franklin E., ***The Negro Church in America***, New York, Shocken Books, 1963.
31. Furst, J. ***Edgar Cayce's Story of Jesus***, New York, 1968.
32. Hill, Napoleon, ***You Can Work Your Own Miracles***, New York, Fawcett Gold Medal Book, Napoleon Hill Foundation, 1977.
33. Holliwell, Raymond, ***Working with the Law***, Atlantic City, New Jersey - School of Christian Philosophy, 1964.
34. Hone, William, ***The Lost Books of the Bible*** , Cleveland, Ohio, 1926, Bell Edition, New York- Bell Publishing Company,1979.
35. Hudson, Geoffrey, ***The Hidden Wisdom in the Holy Bible Vol.I***, Wheaton, Illinois, The Theosophical House, Quest Book Edition, 1969.
36. James, George, G. M., ***Stolen Legacy***, San Francisco, California, Julian Richardson, 1976.
37. Jenkins, Ulysses Duke, ***Ancient African Religion and the African American Church***, Jacksonville, N.C., International, 1978.
38. Johnson, James Weldon, Poem, *The Creation*, ***The Negro Caravan***, New York, Dryden Publishing Company, 1941.
39. Jones, C. C. Rev., ***The Oral Religious Instruction of Negroes in the United States***, Liberty County, Georgia, 1942.
40. Jung, Carl, ***The Undiscovered Self***, New York, New American Library, 1957.
41. Klausner, J., ***From Jesus to Paul***, London, England, 1946.
42. Koestler, Arthur, ***The Thirteenth Tribe***, Palmdale, California, Omni Publications, 1976.
43. Kunjufu, Jawanza, ***Adam Where Are You?***, Chicago, Illinois, African American Images Press, 1994.

44. Lewis. David, H., ***Mysteries of the Pyramids***, St. Petersburg, Florida Science Research Publishing House, 1978.
45. Lincoln, C. Eric, ***The Black Church Since Frazier***, New York, Shocken Books.
46. Lucas, J. ***Olumide, The Religion of the Yorubas***, Lagos, Nigeria, C.M.S. Bookshop, 1948.
47. Mack, B., ***The Lost Gospel: The Book of Q and Christian Origins***, New York, Harper Collins/Shaftesbury, 1993.
48. Mancan, James, T., ***The Secret of Perfect Living***, Hemel Hempstead, England, Herts- Parker Publishing Co., 1963.
49. Monroe, Myles, ***Understanding Your Potential***, Shippenburg, Pennsylvania, Destiny Image Publishers, 1991.
50. Murphy, Joseph M., ***Working the Spirit - Ceremonies of the African Diaspora***, Boston, Massachusetts, Beacon Press, 1994.
51. Murphy, Joseph, ***The Power of Your Subconscious Mind***, New York, Bantam Books, 1963.
52. Murray-Beasley, G.R., ***Baptism in the New Testament***, New York, St. Martin's Press, 1962.
53. *New York Times Newspaper*, New York, November 20, 1924.
54. Notovitch, Nicolas, ***The Unknown Life of Jesus Christ***, New York, 1890.
55. Oduyoye, Modupe, ***The Vocabulary of Yoruba Religious Discourse***, Ibadan, Nigeria, Daystar, 1971.
56. Peck, Scott C., Dr., ***Further Along the Road Less Travelled***, New York, Simon & Schuster, 1993.
57. Potter, Rev., Dr., C.F., ***The Lost Years of Jesus Revealed***, Greenwich, Connecticut, 1962.
58. Rashad, Adib, (James Miller) ***Elijah Muhammad and the Ideological Foundation of the Nation of Islam***, Newport News, Virgin U.B. & U.S. Communications Systems, 1993.
59. Read, Ann, ***Edgar Cayce on Jesus and His Church***, New York, 1970.
60. Sheldon, Charles M. and Garrett W., ***What Would Jesus Do?***, Inspirational Press Books, 1997.
61. Stebbing, Lionel, ***A Dictionary of Occult Science***, London, England, Emerson Press.
62. Tawney, Richard, ***Religion and the Rise of Capitalism***, Peter Smith, New American Library, Mentor Books, 1926.
63. Thompson, Robert, Farris, ***Flash of Spirit: African and Afro-***

American Art and Philosophy, New York Random House, 1983.

64. Thurman, Howard, ***Jesus and the Disinherited***, Boston, Massachusetts, Beacon Press, 1949, originally published by Abingdon Press, New York.
Disciplines of the Spirit, NY Harper and Row 1963 reprinted Richmond, Indiana Friends United Press, 1977.
65. Twum-Barima, Vod, ***Man Know Thyself***, Tema, Ghana Publishing Corp., 1989.
66. Vanzant, Iyanla, Speech given at Union Temple Baptist Church, Washington, DC., 1995.
67. Volney, C. F., Count ***Ruin of Empires***, France, 1792. Reprint Baltimore, Md., Black Classic Press, 1991.
68. Waitley, Dennis, ***Seeds of Greatness***, New York, Simon & Schuster, 1983.
69. Walker, Thomas Rev., Gospel Song, *I'm Only Human*, original country western song, *One Day at a Time*, Ascap Recording Co., Kris Kristofferson.
70. Walker, Williston, ***A History of the Christian Church***, New York, Scribner & Sons, 1918, renewal, Amelia Walker and Elizabeth, 1946.
71. Walls, Bishop J. William, ***The African Methodist Episcopal Zion Church- Reality of the Black Church***, Charlotte, N.C., Amez Publishing House, 1974.
72. Watts, Jill, ***God, Harlem USA- The Father Divine Story***, Berkeley, California, The University of California Press, 1992.
73. Weber, Max, ***The Protestant Ethic and the Spirit of Capitalism***, New York, Charles Scribner, 1958.
74. Welsing, Frances Cress, Dr., Lecture at Union Temple Baptist Church, Washington, D.C., 1991.
75. Wilson, Amos, ***The Falsification of Afrikan Consciousness- Eurocentric History, Psychiatry and the Politics of White Supremacy***, New York, African World Info System, 1993.
76. Wright, Leon, Dr., ***From Cult to Cosmos - Can Jesus Be Saved?***, Petaluma, California by Crystal Press, 1978.